# Jet Li

## Other books in the People in the News series:

Maya Angelou

Tyra Banks

Glenn Beck

David Beckham

Beyoncé

Sandra Bullock

Fidel Castro

Kelly Clarkson

Hillary Clinton

Miley Cyrus

Ellen Degeneres

Johnny Depp

Leonardo DiCaprio

Hilary Duff

Zac Efron

Brett Favre

50 Cent

Jeff Gordon

Al Gore

Tony Hawk

Salma Hayek

Jennifer Hudson

LeBron James

Jay-Z

Derek Jeter

Steve Jobs

Dwayne Johnson

Angelina Jolie

Jonas Brothers

Kim Jong II

Coretta Scott King

Ashton Kutcher

Spike Lee

George Lopez

Tobey Maguire

Eli Manning

John McCain

Barack Obama

Michelle Obama

Apolo Anton Ohno

Danica Patrick

Nancy Pelosi

Katy Perry

Tyler Perry

Queen Latifah

Daniel Radcliffe

Condoleezza Rice

Rihanna

Alex Rodriguez

Derrick Rose

J.K. Rowling

Shakira

Tupac Shakur

Will Smith

Gwen Stefani

Ben Stiller

Hilary Swank

Justin Timberlake

Usher

Denzel Washington

Serena Williams

Oprah Winfrey

# Jet Li

by Michael V. Uschan

**LUCENT BOOKS**
*A part of Gale, Cengage Learning*

GALE
CENGAGE Learning·

Detroit • New York • San Francisco • New Haven, Conn • Waterville, Maine • London

GALE
CENGAGE Learning·

**LIBRARY OF CONGRESS CATALOGING-IN-PUBLICATION DATA**

Uschan, Michael V., 1948-
 Jet Li / by Michael V. Uschan.
  p. cm. -- (People in the news)
  Intorduction: a gentle action hero -- Learning the martial arts -- Li becomes an actor --
Hong Kong movie star -- An international star -- Jet Li the philanthropist.
  Includes bibliographical references and index.
  ISBN 978-1-4205-0731-7 (hardcover)
1. Li, Jet, 1963---Juvenile literature. 2. Motion picture actors and actresses--China--Bi-
ography--Juvenile literature. 3. Martial artists--China--Biography--Juvenile literature. I.
Title.
  PN2878.L34U83 2011
  791.43'028092--dc23
  [B]
                                                                              2011029987

Lucent Books
27500 Drake Rd
Farmington Hills MI 48331

ISBN-13: 978-1-4205-0731-7
ISBN-10: 1-4205-0731-1

Printed in the United States of America
1 2 3 4 5 6 7 15 14 13 12 11

# Contents

Fame and celebrity are alluring. People are drawn to those who walk in fame's spotlight, whether they are known for great accomplishments or for notorious deeds. The lives of the famous pique public interest and attract attention, perhaps because their experiences seem in some ways so different from, yet in other ways so similar to, our own.

Newspapers, magazines, and television regularly capitalize on this fascination with celebrity by running profiles of famous people. For example, television programs such as *Entertainment Tonight* devote all their programming to stories about entertainment and entertainers. Magazines such as *People* fill their pages with stories of the private lives of famous people. Even newspapers, newsmagazines, and television news frequently delve into the lives of well-known personalities. Despite the number of articles and programs, few provide more than a superficial glimpse at their subjects.

Lucent's People in the News series offers young readers a deeper look into the lives of today's newsmakers, the influences that have shaped them, and the impact they have had in their fields of endeavor and on other people's lives. The subjects of the series hail from many disciplines and walks of life. They include authors, musicians, athletes, political leaders, entertainers, entrepreneurs, and others who have made a mark on modern life and who, in many cases, will continue to do so for years to come.

These biographies are more than factual chronicles. Each book emphasizes the contributions, accomplishments, or deeds that have brought fame or notoriety to the individual and shows how that person has influenced modern life. Authors portray their subjects in a realistic, unsentimental light. For example, Bill Gates—cofounder of the software giant Microsoft—has been instrumental in making personal computers the most vital tool of the modern age. Few dispute his business savvy, his perseverance, or his technical expertise, yet critics say he is ruthless in his dealings with competitors and driven more by his desire to maintain Microsoft's dominance in the computer industry than by an interest in furthering technology.

In these books, young readers will encounter inspiring stories about real people who achieved success despite enormous obstacles. Oprah Winfrey—one of the most powerful, most watched, and wealthiest women in television history—spent the first six years of her life in the care of her grandparents while her unwed mother sought work and a better life elsewhere. Her adolescence was colored by pregnancy at age fourteen, rape, and sexual abuse.

Each author documents and supports his or her work with an array of primary and secondary source quotations taken from diaries, letters, speeches, and interviews. All quotes are footnoted to show readers exactly how and where biographers derive their information and provide guidance for further research. The quotations enliven the text by giving readers eyewitness views of the life and accomplishments of each person covered in the People in the News series.

In addition, each book in the series includes photographs, annotated bibliographies, timelines, and comprehensive indexes. For both the casual reader and the student researcher, the People in the News series offers insight into the lives of today's newsmakers—people who shape the way we live, work, and play in the modern age.

# A Gentle Action Hero

In the blockbuster movies that have made him a global celebrity, Jet Li is a whirling, kicking, punching weapon of mass destruction that can routinely defeat any opponent who attacks him. Li has disposed of on-screen adversaries in so many exotic ways with his fists, feet, and weapons, such as swords and staffs, that that even his fellow actors are awed with the creativity he displays while fighting. In 1998 Li costarred in *Lethal Weapon 4* with Mel Gibson and Danny Glover. Before the actors began shooting the movie, Gibson told Li how impressed he was with fight scenes from Li's other films. Gibson even jokingly told Li, "I saw your pictures, I like your fights; just decide how to beat me up."[1]

Even though Gibson and Glover both towered over the diminutive five foot six (1.68 meter), 145-pound (66-kilogram) Li, his victories over them in several film fights appear realistic. As an actor, Li emanates an aura of menace and brutality that makes the characters he plays appear fierce and dangerous. More importantly, Li is an expert in a wide variety of Chinese martial arts. Unlike some action film stars who only pretend to know how to fight, Li began studying such techniques when he was only eight years old. And just four years later, Li was good enough to become a national champion in the People's Republic of China in wushu, the collective name for Chinese martial arts. His fighting movements are so swift, precise, powerful, and authentic that moviegoers easily believe Li can defeat actors he is fighting even though his opponents are bigger and appear stronger physically.

Li is actually such a skillful fighter that he could defeat nearly anyone in a real fight. But despite his fighting prowess, Li is a gentle person who does not believe in using his martial arts ability to hurt anyone. In fact, Li once admitted he has never had to use his fighting skills except in competitions and movies:

> I myself have never been in a fight in real life, nor do I wish to be in one. When someone comes up to me, threatens me, wants to challenge me—I do whatever is possible to avoid conflict. Because it is never worth it.[2]

His disdain for violence stems from fundamental principles that underlie Chinese martial arts as well as Li's belief in Buddhism, an eastern religion. Both of those philosophies have combined to make Li perhaps the gentlest actor to ever become an action hero in movies.

## Li's Gentle Philosophy

Like many martial artists, Li believes most people do not realize the true benefits that can be gained from studying the martial arts. Most movies glorify the ability martial artists have to beat up people, but Li says that is the wrong reason to learn them. Li claims that the only legitimate reason for people to use a martial art is if they are attacked: "Kung fu [another generic term for Chinese martial arts] is a means to build your self-pride rather than to destroy others."[3]

Li says people should study the martial arts to improve their physical fitness, agility, balance, and strength. He believes the dedication students need to become proficient in martial arts can teach them self-discipline and how to work hard to achieve something worthwhile. Li also claims students who study the martial arts will gain greater self-confidence and a better understanding of themselves, both of which he believes should lead them away from using their new skills in a negative way. This is how Li once explained why he believes violence is a bad way to deal with other people:

*Despite his action-hero image, actor Jet Li advocates non-violence and promotes the study of martial arts as a way to improve physical fitness, self-discipline, and confidence.*

All your problems are on the inside, in your heart. The problems aren't from the outside, from other people, so you need to study who you are. Who's 100 percent you? If you understand your inside, then you're not afraid anymore.[4]

His philosophical approach to martial arts fits nicely with Li's Buddhist beliefs. Buddhism is both a religion and a philosophy that stresses people should never do anything to harm another living thing. One of the key principles of Buddhist thought is *karma*, which claims that people are rewarded for the good things they do and punished for the bad things they do. Li explains why karma makes violence a poor choice in almost any situation:

> As a Buddhist, I believe strongly in the concept of karma. What you do will come back to you eventually, as is the universal balance. You can win today, but tomorrow, your choice to use violence will return to you, perhaps in a form ten times stronger.[5]

So even though Li has the skills to beat up almost anyone in the world, he would never use this ability to intimidate people or try to prove he is one of the toughest, most dangerous fighters on the planet.

Those same philosophies, especially Buddhism, have also made Li gentle in other ways. Li in 2000 was offered the starring role in *Crouching Tiger, Hidden Dragon*, a film featuring Chinese martial arts that became a worldwide hit. Li turned down the offer because his wife, Nina, was pregnant with their first child, and he had promised her he would not work while she was pregnant. Li is also a philanthropist who raises money through The One Foundation, a charity dedicated to helping people throughout the world recover from natural disasters, such as earthquakes and tsunamis.

## The Real Jet Li

The philosophies that have shaped Li make him far different from most of the characters he portrays in movies, such as the villain Wah Sing Ku, the Chinese criminal in *Lethal Weapon 4* who keeps trying to kill Gibson and Glover. Li is actually a peaceful person known for making kind and gentle statements during interviews, such as "The strongest weapon is a smile and the best power is love."[6] Thus there is a huge difference between Jet Li in the movies and in real life.

*Chapter 1*

# Learning the Martial Arts

In many martial arts movies, the hero endures a grueling period of training to become a fighter skillful enough to defeat any opponent. Jet Li has played that part in several films. He also lived that role while growing up in Beijing, the capital of the People's Republic of China (PRC). When Li was only eight years old, he was chosen to attend a state-run school to learn the Chinese fighting arts that would eventually propel him to global stardom. Movie heroes usually subject themselves to the arduous, often torturous process of mastering the martial arts because they need to defeat villains who have killed someone they love or stolen something precious from them. The motivation for Li to study the martial arts was different. He wanted to help support his family and to get an education he could not otherwise afford. The training, however, was so hard and rigorous that Li had to sacrifice many pleasures young people enjoy while growing up. This is how Li has characterized his years in martial arts school: "The only word I can use to describe our training is 'bitter.' It was harsh."[7]

Yet the bitterness Li experienced enabled him to help his family survive poverty. It also helped him to eventually become a wealthy and successful actor whose name and face are known around the world.

## A Poor Family

Jet Li was named Li Lian-jie when he was born on April 26, 1963, in Beijing, the capital of the PRC. Li is his family name, but in

China people place their family name first. Lian-jie is a combination of his first name Jie,—which means "festival,"—and his middle name Lian, which is shared by family members born in the same generation. Lian-jie was the youngest of five children—he has two older brothers and two older sisters—but little is known about his siblings or parents because Li, an intensely private person, has never discussed them publicly. The most detailed accounts of Li's family and early life are from a series of essays about his youth that he posted on his website (http://jetli.com). In the first essay, Li explains why he decided to write about his life:

> Let's start at the beginning, since childhood experiences are the events which mold your perspective on the world and your views on spirituality. When I was two years old, my father passed away, so I never knew my father's picture in my mind.[8]

Lian-jie's father was an engineer, a position that would have allowed him to earn a decent income. His death forced Lian-jie's mother to work to support her children. She was only able to get low-paying jobs, such as selling tickets to people boarding trains,

*Li speaks at an event in Taipei, Taiwan, in 2008. The Chinese characters in the background represent Li's given name: Li Lian-jie.*

which made it hard for her to provide enough food and clothing for her children. When Lian-jie began attending Changqiao Primary School of Beijing, the eight-year-old had to wear a pair of pants that originally had belonged to one of his sisters; they had also been worn by other siblings before him. Wearing hand-me-down clothes was embarrassing—other students taunted him for his worn clothing—but Li has written that he had no choice: "We were poor. Eight years old, I wear girls' pants to school. The schoolchildren say, 'Oh, you wear your sister's pants.'"[9] Lian-jie also endured cruel remarks from classmates because he did not have a father.

His mother was overly protective of Lian-jie, who was the youngest in the family and small for his age. Thus the young boy who would grow up to be a martial arts expert and play some of the toughest, most dangerous characters in film could not take part in simple activities most children enjoy because his mother feared he would hurt himself. Lian-jie was not allowed to swim, ice skate, or even ride a bicycle, a skill he did not master until he was a teenager, even though it is a common form of transportation in China. Li explains, with more than a touch of bitterness, how boring his life was because of his mother's fears:

Any risky activity—any kind of exercise that was even slightly dangerous—was off-limits. So while kids my age were out playing in the street, this docile little boy stayed inside. "Don't touch that!" adults would tell me, and it would never occur to me to touch it. "Don't eat that!"—and I would leave it alone.[10]

Lian-jie's mother did not let him begin school until he was eight years old, a year later than most children. When he began attending class, his obedient manner and willingness to work hard made him popular with his teachers. Li once explained that he tried to be a good student "because I don't want my mom to feel sad."[11] At school, Lian-jie was finally able to participate in athletic activities his mother had denied him. When that happened, his natural physical ability quickly opened the door to a new life for him.

# Wushu School

The primary school Lian-jie attended was for grades one through six. During a one-month vacation after his first school year ended in 1971, Lian-jie had to attend a summer school that taught students sports like swimming, basketball, and soccer. Government officials started the school to give students activities that kept them out of trouble when they were not in school. China in this period also was trying to become a world power in sports, so the program allowed officials to spot promising young athletes they could develop into future stars.

Several thousand students from fifteen elementary schools who attended the school were arbitrarily assigned to a sport. Lian-jie was ordered to practice wushu even though he knew nothing about it. Wushu, a combination of the Chinese words "wu" (war) and "shu" (art), is a generic term for Chinese martial arts that include many styles of bare-handed fighting and forms that use weapons, such as

*Young Chinese boys practice a martial arts routine. Li began his study of wushu at a government-run sports school when he was eight years old.*

# Wushu and Kung Fu

The formal name for Chinese martial arts is wushu, a name derived from Mandarin, one of the main Chinese languages. It can also be referred to as *kung fu*, an informal term that refers to any individual skill someone acquires through long and hard work. Wushu is popular around the world. People learn various styles for self-defense or to improve their physical strength and health. Mark Salzman

*Three students practice wushu, which the Chinese practice in order to improve their physical and spiritual health.*

studied wushu for two years while teaching English in the Republic of China. This is a brief explanation of wushu written by Salzman:

> The goal of the wushujia, or wushu expert, is to achieve perfect form and concentration. His movements become instinctive and express a harmony of mind and body that the Chinese believe is crucial to spiritual as well as physical health. The wushujia devotes most of his training time to the practice of taolu, or routines. These are choreographed sequences of movements, 1 to 20 minutes in length, that must be carried out according to strict esthetic, technical and conceptual guidelines. There are hundreds of styles of wushu, ranging from taijiquan [tai chi chuan] to forms of boxing that imitate praying mantises, snakes, eagles, even drunken men. The character of each style differs, though their actual techniques may be similar. Regardless of the style, a good taolu looks fluid, graceful and powerful.

Mark Salzman. "Wushu: Mediation in Motion." *New York Times Magazine*, March 29, 1987, p. 30.

spears, swords, and staffs. Students had to spend two-and-half hours each day learning and practicing the fighting styles. They learned to perform taolus, choreographed routines that lasted several minute. Each taolu had a series of offensive and defensive movements that mimicked fighting, and each movement had to be performed precisely and perfectly. Lian-jie enjoyed wushu, and his innate athletic ability helped him become one of the best students.

When the vacation ended, only twenty students were asked to continue wushu lessons. Lian-jie was very proud he had been chosen to continue: "Being selected out of a thousand made you rather famous in your class. Everybody else had been rejected, but you were special!"[12] However, Lian-jie's joy and pride at his new exalted status wore off quickly because the two hours of hard physical lessons after a full day of school left him with little free time. Three months later, Lian-jie survived another drastic reduction in the number of youths studying wushu when instructors again saw enough promise in the young martial artist to want to continue training him. During the winter, the lessons became a physical ordeal for Lian-jie, and other wushu students because they had to practice outside despite Beijing's frigid winter climate.

After Lian-jie had been learning wushu for a year, the nine-year-old had his first chance to measure himself against other young martial artists in a competition in Jinan, which was 300 miles (482.8 kilometers) away from Beijing. Li has written that traveling to another city was thrilling for a young boy who had never left Beijing or ridden a train: "I remember being very excited about the prospect of riding the train. My mother, however, was heartsick at the thought of her baby going so far away from home."[13] Lian-jie won the award for Excellence, the tournament's top prize.

When the young martial artist returned home, he was chosen to receive advanced wushu instruction with other select students. The extra training took so much time that he only attended regular classes for a half-day. Not long after that, Lian-jie was one of several young martial artists chosen to demonstrate wushu at the Pan-Asian-African-Latin American Table Tennis Championships, which were being held in Beijing. Table tennis, also known as Ping-Pong, is a major sport in China. The Communist country in the 1970s began using sports to connect with other countries

# Communism and Wushu

Communist forces commanded by Mao Zedong won a civil war in 1949 for control of China and established the People's Republic of China (PRC). In creating a Communist nation, Mao centralized control over every aspect of life, including the martial arts. Communists embraced the martial arts as a way to teach citizens fighting skills but tried to eliminate their traditional association with religions like Taoism and Buddhism. The Cultural Revolution in the mid-1960s was a period of violence in which young people known as Red Guards attacked those whom they believed were dangerous to Communism, including members of religious groups.

*Members of the Red Guard march in the mid-1960s while carrying pictures of China's Communist leader, Mao Zedong.*

Buddhist priests in the Shaolin Monastery in Dengfeng had taught martial arts for centuries, and the site was revered as one of China's most historic wushu centers. In 1966, Red Guards attacked the monastery. They destroyed buildings, paraded the remaining five monks through nearby streets with signs that proclaimed them to be enemies of the state, and beat them. Red Guards then forced the monks to leave the monastery and become farm workers. Many other martial artists fled the country to avoid persecution. Martial arts for a short time were considered one of the old traditions that had kept China weak, and no wushu competitions were held. China's stance toward wushu softened after the Cultural Revolution ended in 1968. In 1972, when nine-year-old Jet Li won his first wushu competition in Jinan, it was during the first national wushu tournament since the Cultural Revolution.

socially and culturally after having been isolated from the rest of the world for several decades due to differences over political and economic ideals. Lian-jie and the other athletes worked hard for weeks so that their martial arts demonstrations would be flawless. The students performed so well that they were invited to meet afterward with Zhou En-lai, China's prime minister. Li remembers how proud the experience made him feel:

> Just imagine: to be chosen to represent your country with [wushu] and to meet the leader of your country—and then to hear him praise you for your performance. That was an indescribable honor in China, not to mention a thrilling experience for a 9-year old boy.[14]

Lian-jie's brilliant performance led to an invitation to train full-time at the Beijing Sports and Exercise School, which was reserved for China's top athletes. He would even live there during the week so he could concentrate on wushu. Although attending the elite school meant Lian-jie would only see his family one day a week, he realized it was an opportunity he could not pass up: "I was from a very poor family and we didn't have enough money for a good school so sports-school was good; it gave me good food and an opportunity to [eventually] go out of China."[15] At the school he would be fed well, provided with clothes, and receive a small amount of money he could use to help his family.

The young boy's martial arts ability gave him the chance to attend a school that would dramatically change his future. It also immersed Lian-jie in the study of fighting forms that had been evolving in his country for thousands of years.

## A Harsh New Life

The Chinese have been practicing martial arts for self-defense and war for several thousand years. Illustrations on bronze vessels from 1000 B.C. are engraved with figures performing martial arts exercises, and sixteenth-century military leader Ch'i Chi-kuang said he taught fighting skills to his soldiers because "lively hands and feet and a practiced body are a gateway for beginners to enter the art [of making war]."[16] Wushu was revered in China, and students were expected to work extremely hard and dedicate themselves totally to learning the various fighting forms. Thus, life at the sports school was extremely difficult. Lian-jie and other students practiced wushu six days a week, spending so much time learning that they did not have to time to attend regular school. He was allowed to go home Saturday night but had to return early Monday morning for another week of study. This is how Li has described the harsh training regimen of his youth, which began with the ringing of a loud bell at 6 A.M.:

> Within 90 seconds, we had to get dressed and line up outside in the field, standing at attention. After one hour of practice, we had the chance to brush our teeth, wash our face, and eat breakfast. Practice resumed at 8:30 a.m. and lasted until 12 noon. After lunch, we would get the chance to rest for a while.[17]

Although students were supposed to rest after lunch, they often had to perform for tourists who visited the school, which had become famous for the excellence of its martial arts students. Students practiced again in the afternoon, ate dinner at 7:30 P.M., and then practiced again before going to bed. It was hard work physically and mentally because students had to learn so many types of wushu. Lian-jie, however, enjoyed the challenge: "You have hundreds of styles: monkey-style, tiger-style, short sword, hard, longer, many kinds. So today you're learning this. Tomorrow you're learning [something else]. Very interesting."[18] Many fighting styles took their names from animals, both real and imaginary, such as snake, dragon, and praying mantis, because the forms mimicked movements the animals might make.

Wushu teachers were very demanding. For example, they forced students to train outside every day even during the winter when it was bitterly cold or snowing. Teachers would hit students if they were not trying hard enough or were doing a poor job of performing movements of the various styles of fighting. Teachers also refused to accept any excuses for not practicing, even physical injuries. One Friday night when teachers ordered students to

*Chinese youth practice a precise routine at a wushu school in Dengfeng. Li attended a similar school as a young boy, where his study of martial arts was rigorous and demanding.*

run laps outside around a track in the dark, Lian-jie hurt his foot. Despite the injury, he limped around the track and made it through the next day's training on the injured foot before going home. Lian-jie was still in a lot of pain when he returned on Monday. He tried to practice, but an instructor noticed his injury and sent him to a hospital, where X-rays showed he had a broken bone in his foot. However, Lian-jie's teachers would not excuse him from practicing despite the severe injury. Li explained what happened:

> For the next few weeks, an older classmate would carry me on piggyback to the [practice] field every day. He would set me down, and I'd stand there practicing arm movements all day. One thousand, two thousand. No one was allowed to leave the training grounds—that was the rule! When practice ended, the classmate would hoist me onto his back and carry me back to the dorms. That's how it was for several weeks as my leg healed.[19]

Not all teachers were mean. One teacher even became like the father Lian-jie had never known.

# He Had To Keep Training

**W**hen Li Liang-jie broke a bone in his foot while he studied at the Beijing Sports and Exercise School, he did not complain to his coaches even though the injury was very painful. In an essay on his life, Jet Li explains why he did not bring the injury to the attention of his coaches:

> Because we had discovered long ago that complaining about an injury would cause the coach to assign you some new hellacious set of exercises that made you wish you'd never spoken up in the first place. Say, for example, a student told him that she'd hurt her arm—could she take a break from practice? "Hmm," he would say. "You're right. You shouldn't overwork your arm. Why don't you work on leg exercises instead?" Two thousand kicks, or maybe five thousand stances. Whatever reason you came up with to shirk training, the coach was ready with ten alternatives to counter you. He didn't care whether the injury was real or faked. All that mattered was that he would find some exercise involving another part of your body. "Your knee hurts? Okay, you don't have to run. Do a thousand sit-ups instead." The new assignment would leave you in greater pain than actually running on the bad knee. Complaining only made things worse for yourself. You vowed to keep your mouth shut in the future.

Jet Li. "Life Essay: Part 4." The Official Jet Li Website. http://jetli.com/jet/index.php?l=en&s=life&ss=essays&p=4.

## A Father Figure

Wu Bin was the school's most famous teacher. Wu could be harsh but he could also be kind to his pupils. When Wu asked Lian-jie why he did not seem to have enough strength to do some of the martial arts movements, the young boy told him his mother could not afford to buy meat to feed him. Wu began giving Lian-jie's mother money so she could buy meat to make her son strong.

In 1972, when Lian-jie hurt his kneecap and was confined to bed, his mother begged him to quit wushu. She told her son "Look here, little Jie, to practice wushu you need extra nutrition. But we simply can't afford the expenses [and] I think you'd better stop training." When Wu visited the injured boy, Lian-jie told him he was going to quit the martial arts. Wu was disappointed but told him that whatever decision he made he should "be a brave boy and not a coward." The words inspired Lian-jie to return to the school and keep learning wushu:

> After this incident, I came to understand that one should not leave anything half done. I thereafter I practiced extra hard. What my teammates did once in a training session I did thrice. To make the most of my time, I worked in the gym even on Sundays, when everybody else was resting.[20]

*Young Chinese boys pause during their wushu practice. Li's study of the martial arts as a young boy often required him to work through injury and fatigue in order to keep up with his teachers' high expectations of him.*

Wu, however, did not always treat Lian-jie with kindness. He saw so much athletic ability and promise of greatness in the young boy that he was more critical and demanding of him than of his other students. Although Wu sometimes allowed students to rest if they looked tired, he usually ignored signs of fatigue in Lian-jie and made him keep working. Wu would also ridicule the way the young boy performed his wushu and tell Lian-jie he was getting worse, even though the boy was practicing more than anyone else. As an adult, Li has admitted that he often hated how Wu treated him. But Li also acknowledged that Wu kept badgering him because the teacher knew it was the best way to make Li work hard and improve: "Seeing that I was [a] willing trainee, he applied the rigorous method of training toward me. This was described by him as 'A resounding drum must be struck with a heavy hammer.'"[21] Liang-jie would soon reward his mentor's interest by becoming a national wushu champion.

## A Young Champion

In 1974 Lian-jie competed in the Youth National Athletic Competition for wushu athletes younger than eighteen. Three years of intense training and his natural ability allowed the eleven-year-old to dominate the event. Lian-jie won the overall championship by getting the highest marks of all contestants in several events, including demonstrating how to fight with a sword and two-man sparring. He was so much younger than other competitors that he became a celebrity in China. His victory led to his being named to the prestigious Beijing Wushu Team, which toured the United States later that year.

Being able to represent China in another country was a huge honor. But as an adult, Li explained that his motivation to be a top martial artist was greater than just earning personal glory. Li said he wanted to master wushu to help support his mother, brothers, and sisters: "I can take care of them. This is why I train very hard."[22] Such dedication would ultimately propel him to movie stardom and riches beyond his wildest dreams.

# Chapter 2

# Li Becomes
# an Actor

The People's Republic of China (PRC) and the United States became political and economic enemies after Communists won control of China in 1949, following a civil war for control of the country. The two nations fought each other in the Korean War (1950–1953), and there were no formal diplomatic relations between the two powerful nations for nearly two decades. Chinese officials would not even allow Americans to visit their country. But in 1971, China decided to resume relations with the United States. In what was considered a bold diplomatic move, China invited fifteen U.S. Ping-Pong players who were competing in a tournament in Japan to visit Beijing. On April 6, 1971, the team and three journalists accompanying them became the first U.S. citizens to enter China in twenty-two years. Ping-Pong was and is immensely popular in China, and 18,000 people gathered at Tsinghua University to watch the friendly matches between U. S. and Chinese players. Afterward Chinese Premier Chou En-lai claimed, "Never before in history has a sport been used so effectively as a tool of international diplomacy."[23] The sports diplomacy led a year later to President Richard M. Nixon's historic visit to China and a meeting with Mao Zedong, who had led the Communists to power and was still the nation's most powerful official.

The Ping-Pong initiative was so successful that China began using other sports exchanges to strengthen its relationship the United States. The result of that diplomatic effort was a historic encounter between Li Liang-jie and Nixon that made the eleven-year-old a hero in China.

*A Chinese ping-pong player, left, trains a member of the American ping-pong team during its historic visit to China in 1971, a trip that was considered important to establishing diplomatic ties between the two nations.*

## A Trip to the United States

In 1974 Liang-jie was one of thirty young athletes who traveled to the United States to demonstrate Chinese martial arts. To prepare for the trip, students practiced their wushu harder to make sure their performances would be perfect. They also had to learn how to behave socially in a foreign country because none of them had traveled outside China. For six months, students had lessons in etiquette and English to prepare for social situations in the United States. They even had to learn a new way to eat because people in China use chopsticks to pick up food instead of silverware. Li explained the rigorous training students endured:

> Not only were we taught how to eat with a knife and a fork, but we had to know which knife and fork were used for each course. We were taught the proper protocol for answering

the telephone, how to listen and respond when an American asked us a question, how we were expected to behave when surrounded by crowds.[24]

The first stop on the goodwill tour was Mexico. The group then backtracked to Hawaii, where Lian-jie set foot on U.S. soil for the first time when his plane landed at Honolulu International Airport. The young boy remembers being excited at seeing an airplane with "China Airlines" written on it. But when Liang-jie happily commented about the airplane, an adult chaperone angrily told him to be quiet. The plane was from an airline operated by the Republic of China, a country also known as Taiwan, located on a large island near the PRC. Taiwan was founded by political leaders the Communists had defeated in the civil war for control of China. Liang-jie knew right away he had made a serious mistake by mentioning the airline from his country's most hated enemy: "When the adults hushed me, I quickly realized that I'd done something wrong. I was scared to death. Thought they'd send me back home for sure."[25] Luckily, his only punishment was angry looks from chaperones.

*Chinese wushu students give a performance to showcase their skills. Li was only eleven years old when he toured the United States with a team of other young martial artists and performed for President Richard Nixon.*

# A Naughty Boy

Jet Li admits he was a meek, well-behaved little boy while growing up. However, he has written that during his 1974 trip to the United States he began doing things even though he knew he should not be doing them. One of them was teasing a Chinese bodyguard who escorted him everywhere he went:

> I was growing up ... and I was becoming mischievous. [I] was fascinated with the guns that the bodyguards carried. Despite the fact that the guards were officially discouraged from speaking to us, I kept asking the guys if I could look at their guns up close and maybe hold them. I especially remember that I was always trying to joke around with my own bodyguard. Because I was short for my age and only came up mid-torso, I'd gotten into the habit of holding on to his shirt as we walked. He would walk in front and I would tag along behind him. My height gave me excellent access to his belt, which is of course exactly where his holster was located. "Hey, cool!" I'd say as I reached out to touch his gun, and he'd tense up. I believe I did this at least once every day. Such nice memories!

Jet Li. "Life Essay: Part 6." The Official Jet Li Website. http://jetli.com/jet/index.php?l=e n&s=life&ss=essays&p=6

The thirty young martial artists who traveled to Mexico, Honolulu, San Francisco, New York, and Washington, D.C., were accompanied by fourteen adult chaperones and twenty-six military intelligence bodyguards. The youths were guarded so heavily because Chinese officials wanted to prevent any negative incidents that could embarrass their country. U.S. security officials also provided police escorts and guards and monitored every move the Chinese made. This surveillance extended to placing listening devices in their rooms.

Liang-jie thought it was funny when adults in his group warned him that his hotel room would have listening devices. Although Liang-jie had been a shy, polite little boy who never did anything to upset his teachers or mother, he had become mischievous as his confidence had grown due to his martial arts success. When the group arrived in New York, the eleven-year-old decided to test whether anyone was really listening to him. Because he did not know where the devices were hidden, he talked randomly to various objects:

> One day, feeling silly, I faced the telephone (without picking it up) and said, "Hey, I want chocolate, I want chocolate, I want chocolate." Then I turned to the mirror and said: "I want ice cream, ice cream, ice cream, ice cream." Lastly, I ran over to the flower vase and said: "I want banana, I want banana, I want banana."[26]

When Liang-jie returned to his room that night after a martial arts performance, he was shocked to see that the items he mentioned had been delivered to his room. The unexpected delivery frightened him, and he never joked with the secret listeners again.

The final stop on the tour was Washington, D.C., the nation's capital, and a scheduled meeting with President Nixon.

## Lian-jie Meets Nixon

On a warm, sunny day in July, Liang-jie and several other Chinese martial artists demonstrated wushu on the lawn outside the White House for President Nixon, Secretary of State Henry Kissinger, and a small group of newspaper and television reporters. Nixon and Kissinger posed for a photograph with the students, who were wearing loose-fitting red shirts and pants. A girl with a pink bow in her hair handed Nixon some flowers and then performed one of the choreographed routines wushu martial artists practice.

The slight young girl's graceful, acrobatic movements probably seemed more like ballet or gymnastics than a style of fighting to the Americans. But when Liang-jie and Chu Shi-fai performed a two-man routine, everyone could see the deadly intent of each move the young boys made to either attack an opponent or to block a blow or kick.

Although it might have seemed frivolous for the president of the world's most powerful nation to take time from his busy schedule to watch young martial artists, Nixon's comments after the performance showed how important it had been. Nixon claimed the visit by the martial arts troupe would help strengthen the growing friendly relationship between two nations who had been enemies for many years. Nixon told the young martial artists, "This [demonstrates] the basic friendship between the Chinese people and Americans. You will make many friends for the Chinese people."[27]

*President Richard Nixon, left, meets with Chinese premier Chou-En-Lai during a historic trip to China in 1972. Li met the president when he visited the United States in 1974 as part of a Chinese contingent of martial artists who performed at the White House.*

Nixon praised Lian-jie for his fighting ability and jokingly asked him to become his bodyguard when he grew up. To Nixon's surprise, the eleven-year-old gave a serious response to his light-hearted quip, saying, "I don't want to protect any individual. When I grow up, I want to defend my one billion Chinese countrymen."[28] Kissinger then told Lian-jie "Little boy, when you grow up, you should become a diplomat instead of a bodyguard."[29] Kissinger's help in arranging Nixon's 1972 trip and helping China and the United States resume normal relations had made him famous for his diplomacy.

Lian-jie's bold comment to the president was widely reported in the news media in China and around the world. Although many Americans thought the little boy's answer was cute, people in China were intensely proud that Lian-jie had the courage to answer the president of the United States as he did. He became a hero for his patriotism. When Lian-jie returned home, his celebrity continued to grow because of his martial arts prowess.

## Wushu Champion

During their U.S. tour, Chinese officials had given each of the martial arts students $5 a day to buy whatever they wanted. Lian-jie purchased a Swiss watch for his mother, who would never have been able to afford such a fine timepiece. When Lian-jie gave it to her, he said, "She hugged me and said I was a good boy."[30] Being able to buy the watch made Lian-jie realize more than ever that his wushu ability was the surest way he could help his family financially. He began practicing even harder to improve his martial arts skill.

In 1975 Liang-jie entered the wushu competition in the Third National Games, a Chinese version of the Olympics that included a wide variety of sports. This time, the short, slight, twelve-year-old martial artist had to compete against adults and not youngsters his own age. In the intensive training leading up to the competition in Beijing, Lian-jie cut his head so badly doing a solo routine that he needed stitches to close the wound. That severe injury, however, could not stop him from competing. Although

Liang-jie had to wear a bandage to cover the wound, he tore it off during the competition while performing wushu routines or sparring with an opponent. Lian-jie was a foot shorter and a decade younger than some of his competitors. But incredibly, he scored the highest marks in the events that he was named Men's All-Around National Champion.

As the Chinese national anthem played while Lian-jie was being honored for his victory, the young boy thought to himself of his mother and how he had trained hard to make her proud of him: "This medal is for you, Mom! You didn't raise me in vain! Without your sacrifices, I couldn't have made it to this point."[31] The national championship was the first of five consecutive titles the young martial artist would win to make his mother proud of him.

Li was able to dominate his sport partly because of his physical prowess, especially his jumping ability and the quickness with which he performed kicks, hand strikes, and other movements. His greatest attribute was speed, which led his fellow students to nickname him "Jet." But Li also won the titles because he worked so hard to master wushu styles and was able to use his mind and creativity to combine elements of the various styles into his own personal fighting style. Li even invented a new way to train his body. He used ropes to suspend soccer balls between trees and then engaged in an exercise he named "Beating Stars." He hit or kicked the balls to make them bounce back and forth and then kept striking the constantly moving targets with his hands and feet. Li explained that in this training method, "One attacks from all four sides and protects from four sides too. It practices the hands, eyes, body and feet to be swift and fast, turning and responding."[32]

As China's national champion, Li in the next few years traveled with other martial artists throughout Asia, Europe, and the Middle East to showcase Chinese wushu. In a 1976 stop in Afghanistan, it was so hot that Li and his companions had to pour water on the sheets of their beds so their bodies would be cool enough to sleep. The heat was also fierce during a 1977 stop in an African country. When Li reached into an ice-filled barrel for a cool drink during a martial arts demonstration, he retrieved a small bottle and drank

*An adult Li strikes an imposing stance to demonstrate his mastery of the martial arts. As a teen, Li was China's national wushu champion, and he toured Asia, Europe, and the Middle East extensively to demonstrate his skills.*

half of it so fast he did not taste it. When Li began feeling dizzy, he realized the bottle had contained champagne: "I was no good to perform after that, so they had to find somebody to replace me that night."[33] And when important officials such as U. S. Presidents Gerald Ford and Jimmy Carter visited China, Li was always asked to greet them because of his famous meeting with Nixon.

# A New Image of America

L i Liang-jie's trip to the United States in 1974 with other martial artists drastically changed the way he viewed America and its citizens. People who lived in the People's Republic of China and United States knew little about each other because they had never met people from the other country or visited there. Cultural exchanges like the visit by martial artists were important because it helped Chinese athletes learn about the United States and people who saw their demonstrations learn something about China. Li comments on how his attitude about the United States changed because of what he experienced during the trip:

> Back in school, we'd been educated to think: "China is good. Everything in China is good," and "The Western countries are decadent societies. Everything about America is evil." When we actually found ourselves walking around in this Western country, however, we couldn't help but notice how different everything was from China—and not necessarily in a bad way. "Wow, there are so many cars here. Hey, look at those tall buildings! Geez, Americans actually have swimming pools in their backyards!" There were so many new "wow"s every day. None of us dared say the words—"Hey, it's pretty nice here!"—but everybody was thinking it.

William Nakayama. "Jet Li: The Chosen." *Goldsea Asian American Daily.* http://goldsea.com/Personalities/Lijet/lijet.html.

Li worked hard to become China's best martial artist. But he admitted years later that his success became a burden to him: "I felt like I was carrying a lot of responsibility. I felt like I was representing a billion people and needed to do good."[34] Another price Li paid to be a wushu champion were injuries he suffered during his intensive training and competition. He was able to cope with a variety of physical ailments until 1979, when he tore the anterior cruciate ligament (ACL) in his knee while doing a jump kick.

The injury was so severe that Li had to retire from wushu competition. Luckily, the fame and success Li had enjoyed allowed him to do something even more enjoyable and rewarding than being a symbol to the world of Chinese martial arts. At age sixteen, Li finally said yes to film producers who had long wanted him to star in a movie.

## Jet Li and Bruce Lee

After Li's historic White House appearance in 1974, the last stop for the wushu students before returning home was Hong Kong. There, Li saw his first movie starring Bruce Lee, whose martial arts prowess and screen charisma had helped make martial arts movies popular around the world. Years later, Li admitted that seeing Lee had profoundly affected him:

> I remember watching that movie when I was 11 and just being amazed. What I couldn't believe was how Bruce moved in that movie. He obviously trained in the traditional Chinese martial arts as I did. To this day, he is the only other actor who has ever used that kind of martial arts in the movies.[35]

Lee was born in San Francisco but grew up in Hong Kong, where he learned the martial arts. Hong Kong movie studios had been making low-budget movies featuring the martial arts for years, but they had never been popular outside of Asia. Lee's dynamic screen personality in films such as *The Big Boss* (1971) and *Fist of Fury* (1972) made them the most successful Hong Kong films ever, and in 1973 Lee became an international star in *Enter the Dragon*, which was filmed in cooperation with Warner Brothers, a Hollywood studio.

When Lee died in May 1973 while shooting *Game of Death*, Hong Kong film studios began searching for new stars to replace

*Legendary Chinese American martial artist Bruce Lee performs in the 1973 movie* Enter the Dragon, *which made him an international star. Lee's skill and success was a big influence on young Li.*

him. Because Li was famous for his meeting with Nixon and his many wushu titles, Hong Kong producers contacted him several times about acting in films. The first time was during Li's 1974 visit to Hong Kong, when he was only eleven years old. Li kept declining such offers until 1979 because he did not think he was ready to act in a film. But in 1979, the sixteen-year-old wushu champion finally said yes. Li knew he had the martial arts ability to act in such movies. He also believed that his experience in performing in front of live audiences and news cameras for nearly

## A Good Movie

*The Shaolin Temple* instantly transformed Jet Li into a movie star. When the movie opened in the People's Republic of China and Hong Kong in 1982 even *Variety*, the weekly bible of entertainment news based in New York, took note of the movie shot in far-off China. In its review of the film, the newspaper praised Li's rookie performance: "He has verve, youth, charm, humor and [performs] marvelous athletic feats yet is without the cockiness of a Cantonese stunt man turned kung-fu star." The final comment was the reviewer's realization that unlike some actors who only pretend to know the martial arts, the business-like way Li fought showed that he was a true master of wushu. The review said the film was superior to most films in the kung fu genre because of the honest way it portrayed the martial arts:

> A kung-fu picture is a kung-fu picture, but here's something different. While the Shaolin Temple idea has been done to death the plot gives opportunities to show off unique and exotic kung-fu techniques not seen before in the countless cheapies that dominated the local screens. The difference lies in the presentation of the martial arts.

James Robert Parish. *Jet Li: A Biography*. New York: Thunder's Mouth Press, 2002, p. 41.

a decade while touring the world had also prepared him for an acting career. This is how Li once explained why he believed he could become a successful actor:

> From the beginning I learned martial arts, and from that I became an actor. I had to learn a lot about acting [but in] Chinese there's a saying that doesn't translate very well, that life is the acting, acting is the life.[36]

His first movie was *The Shaolin Temple*. It would change his life.

## Shaolin Temple

The movie released in 1982 was historic because it was the first martial arts film made in the People's Republic of China. It was also the first filmed on location at the Shaolin Temple, an ancient Buddhist monastery in Hunan Province that is revered as the birthplace of China's most famous wushu style. For 1,500 years, monks there had practiced fighting styles based on the movements of animals and birds that became known as Shaolin kung fu. The ancient monastery provided a vivid, authentic backdrop for the movie even though it was in disrepair after long neglect. Both firsts were possible because the Chinese government was edging toward business deals with other countries to strengthen its weak economy. To make the movie, China entered into a partnership with Chung Yuen Motion Picture Company, a Hong Kong movie studio. Hong Kong at the time was controlled by Great Britain, but in 1997 it became a part of China.

The movie is set in the seventh century. Li plays Jue Yuan, who wants to learn martial arts so he can kill Wang, an evil warlord who murdered his father. It took more than two years to shoot the low-budget film due to primitive production methods and several delays, including time in which work was suspended because Li fractured a leg while filming a fight scene. Despite long, arduous days of shooting, Li claimed that making the film was like being on vacation compared to practicing and learning wushu:

> The best part about making that movie was that we didn't have to train anymore. Even though we were waking up at

*Lights lend a glow to the entrance gate to the historic Shaolin Temple, an ancient Buddhist monastery that is considered the birthplace of kung fu. Li's first movie, made in 1982, was named after and filmed on location at the site.*

5 or 6 to get to the set, and shooting from 8 until sunset, it was nothing. This was relaxing. Didn't we have to fight all day? Sure, but this was nowhere near as tiring as wushu class. In fact, after we finished the day's shoot, we'd go out again and play soccer or basketball.[37]

The movie became a huge hit throughout Asia, and its spectacular fight scenes made Li a star. The movie also resulted in Li Lian-jie getting a new name. Theater owners who thought his first and middle names were too long for posters or theater marquees began using his nickname "Jet." Thus was born the actor known as Jet Li.

# Chapter 3

# Hong Kong Movie Star

In the first month after *Shaolin Temple* was released in the winter of 1982, more than 700,000 people in Hong Kong flocked to theaters to see it. The teenage actor impressed moviegoers throughout Asia with the authentic martial arts ability he displayed in fight scenes. The wide-eyed innocence and charm he radiated naturally on screen made them like him even more. Fans began mobbing Li at personal appearances, and some even traveled to his Beijing home in hopes of meeting or seeing him. In a documentary on his life titled *Li-Thal Weapon*, Li explained that movie fame in the People's Republic of China (PRC), much like fame everywhere, came with a personal price:

> When the film came the whole country went mad. Everyone saw the film, from children to grandparents. Soon my face was everywhere; soon everyone knew who I was. I enjoyed the fame but there were some sacrifices I had to make. I couldn't go out shopping and stuff ordinary people do. I ended up staying at home a lot.[38]

Besides fame and adulation, his experience making the movie gave Li a new purpose in his life. He loved the martial arts and believed they were beneficial in helping people improve their health and learn important lessons such as discipline. Li once said:

> I started by making one movie. My eyes just opened. I saw a lot of people watching the movie, and they started liking

# Shaolin Temple

The Shaolin Temple has been revered for 1,500 years as the birthplace of Buddhism and some of some of China's most important styles of martial arts. Bodhidharma, a famous Buddhist monk from India, visited the temple in 527 and founded Chan Buddhism, which is known in Japan as Zen Buddhism. Bodhidharma developed exercises for monks that mimicked the movement of

*A fresco painted from the ancient Shaolin Temple depicts monks practicing kung fu, which originated at the historic site.*

animals that eventually evolved into styles of fighting. During the Cultural Revolution in the 1960s, Red Guards attacked the monastery as part of their campaign against religion. They destroyed some of the monastery's ancient artifacts and beat and ridiculed five monks who lived there. Less than two decades later, People's Republic of China officials, who had condoned violence against a site sacred to Buddhists and martial artists, allowed the monastery to be used in three movies starring Li. The monastery's ancient buildings and murals delighted moviegoers and reawakened interest in the temple and its history. The Shaolin Temple became a popular tourist site, and many martial arts schools opened near it. Li once commented on the amazing transformation the Shaolin movies caused in the temple's fortunes: "When I was working in Shaolin there were [only] three monks and not a lot of people knew about the Shaolin Temple. After the movie came out it became very popular. A lot of tourists, a lot of martial arts schools."

Martha Burr, "Big Jet Li Interview." Kungfu, November 2001. www.kungfumagazine. com/magazine/article.php?article=143.

the martial arts. Then I said, why not just continue making movies, and through the movies give out more information. I really wanted the martial arts to help people.[39]

It was easy for Li to continue acting because the Chung Yuen Motion Picture Company had signed him to a contract for two more films. Li starred in two follow-ups to *Shaolin Temple*, neither of which matched the success of his smash debut. Thus began a period of several years in which Li struggled to become a major martial-arts movie star. Li even moved briefly to the United States to achieve that goal before returning to Hong Kong to star in films that finally propelled him to the fame and fortune he was seeking.

# Unhappy Making Movies

The Hong Kong film company tried to capitalize on the success of Li's first movie in 1984 with *Shaolin Temple 2: Kids from Shaolin* and in 1986 with *Shaolin Temple 3: Martial Arts of Shaolin*. The films were billed as sequels, but the only connection to the original movie was the word "Shaolin" in their titles. In the second film, Li played one of eight orphaned boys raised by a Shaolin monk who taught them secret fighting techniques. A second family with eight sisters who were also martial artists, lived nearby. The two families, however, were enemies because each family believed its style of fighting was superior. In a movie filled with broad comedy, the young men and women battle each other whenever they meet, gradually begin to fall in love, and then band together to fight an evil warlord who is terrorizing the area.

Although Li enjoyed making movies, working conditions were terrible. Li claimed that during the ten months it took to shoot the second Shaolin film in southern China "We lived like the poorest peasants." Cast and crew members sometimes camped out at film locations, had no running water, and ate poorly prepared food. In addition, temperatures as high as 104 degrees endangered actors because there was no air conditioning to let them recover from the oppressive heat. Li said "It was not uncommon for one of us to go into shock from the heat. You'd be fighting, and suddenly somebody would topple over. Somebody would revive us and then we'd have go shoot the scene again."[40]

The third movie was an even more horrible experience for Li. Although most workers on his first two films had been from the PRC, director Lau Ka-leung brought in many actors and workers from Hong Kong. Lau discriminated against PRC Chinese in many ways, from paying them less than Hong Kong workers—Li himself received only $1,500, only twice what he got for his first two films even though he had become a major star in such films—to showing no respect for their talents. The twenty-two-year-old actor was also angry that Lau would not let him suggest his ideas for the plot or how fight scenes should be shot, something other directors had allowed him. Li believed movies should tell a worthwhile story and not be just a series of fights stitched together by an unbelievable, often silly plot, which was the case in that film.

The bitter experience made Li question whether he wanted to continue making movies. When Hong Kong film companies learned Li was considering quitting, they made him several offers to continue because they believed he could be a big star. One proposition was so enticing that Li accepted it. For the first time, Li would direct as well as star in a movie.

*Li's handprints and signature are preserved along Hong Kong's Avenue of the Stars in Kowloon. Although he eventually became an international superstar, he endured low pay and poor working conditions in the early years of his career.*

# Jet Li Demands Respect

Jet Li was unhappy making the third Shaolin Temple movie because director Lau Ka-leung treated actors and workers from the People's Republic of China with less respect than he did those from Hong Kong. The incident that bothered Li the most occurred when Lau scheduled a 3 A.M. shooting time but did not show up until 10 A.M., at which time he called off the day's shooting. This is what Li said when he complained to the movie's producer about the incident:

> I may not know much about making movies. I've only made two, and I'm very young. So can I ask you a simple question? If the shot list calls for a scene to be shot at daybreak and the crew is ready at 3:00 a.m., and then the director shows up at 10:00 a.m. and says the light's all wrong, is he wrong or am I? If you say I'm wrong, then I guess I really don't understand this industry, in which case I promise to go back home right now and never make another movie. On the other hand if you think the director's the one who needs to learn something about filmmaking, then maybe you'll agree that he owes the entire cast and crew an apology.

Li's willingness to stand up for what he believed led the producer to order the director to apologize to Li and the other actors.

William Nakayama, "Jet Li: The Chosen." *Goldsea Asian American Daily*, http://goldsea.com/Personalities/Lijet/lijet.html.

## Li's Life Changes

Li had first become famous in China for his patriotic response in 1974 to President Nixon's whimsical request that the eleven-year-old should consider becoming his bodyguard when he grew up. In *Born to Defense*, Li once again displayed his love for his country. In the 1986 movie, Li plays "Jet," a Chinese soldier who returns home from fighting the Japanese after World War II. He learns to his dismay that U.S. sailors who had been fighting the Japanese now control criminal activities in the port city; they have even forced the daughter of a friend into prostitution. "Jet" begins a series of battles with crooked sailors to rescue the girl and defend other Chinese people they are bullying.

The movie about the relations between Chinese citizens and foreigners like people from the United States has been a touchy subject in China for a very long time. Until Communists won control of the country in 1949, China had been dominated economically and politically for more than a century by nations, such as Japan, Great Britain, and the United States. Li wanted the movie to be a thrilling depiction of martial arts, but also a symbolic statement that Chinese people would no longer tolerate being bullied by other nations. Despite its excellent fight scenes, including the finale in which Jet defeats a huge, brutal sailor, the film was not very good. Bret Fetzer was one of many film critics who gave the movie an unkind review: "It's a good thing Li hasn't quit acting; the script is pure melodrama and Li's fledgling direction doesn't rise above that."[41]

*Li, right, gets the best of a U.S. sailor in a fight scene from the 1986 movie* Born to Defense, *a patriotic film in which the Chinese triumph over foreign bullies.*

The film made Li realize he was not suited to be a director, so he decided to return to acting. This time, however, Li wanted to go to the United States where salaries were far higher and working conditions better. He was probably inspired by Hong Kong martial arts star Jackie Chan, who earned $1 million in 1980 for starring in the Hollywood picture *The Big Brawl*. Money had become more important to Li because in 1987 he had married Huang Qiuyan, a member of his Beijing wushu team whom he had known for years.

As a member of China's national wushu team since childhood, Li had lived a sheltered life. Li was so shy in courting women that he once stood outside a young girl's house for seven hours while holding flowers; he was so frightened he did not have the courage to knock on the door to see if she was home. Li describes the embarrassing end to his attempt at romance: "Finally, her mother came out, took the flowers and went back inside."[42] The way Li became involved with Huang was also inept. Huang was two years older than Li, and he said he began dating her because she was nice to him: "My family was poor. Her family was well-off. She often took care of me [with financial assistance]. That's how it happened. I didn't know what love was."[43] To repay Huang for her kindness, Li even arranged a part for her in his second Shaolin picture; she played the sister he fought and fell in love with.

Li once claimed that he finally decided to marry Huang on the advice of his godmother as a way to change his luck. The Chinese superstition of "chong xi" claims that a happy occasion like a marriage can chase away misfortune a person is experiencing. Li would also soon try to change his luck by moving to the United States. However, neither the move nor the marriage would bring him the good luck he was seeking or last very long.

## Failure in the United States

In 1988 the Chinese government granted Li a two-year exit visa to work in the United States, and he and his wife moved to San Francisco. Li tried to start a movie career, but he failed to win a part in any American-made movies because of his poor English and the lack of parts for Asian actors, even skilled martial artists such as himself. That forced Li to accept the lead role in *Dragon Fight*, a low-budget film financed by a Hong Kong studio that was shot in San Francisco. Li's character was Lap, a Chinese martial artist who becomes stranded in the United States after he is mistakenly accused of killing a policeman. In the movie, Nina Li Chi plays a Chinese woman who helps Li avoid being arrested. The climactic ending has Li defeating a fellow Chinese martial artist who had killed the policeman because he did not want to return to China.

Li biographer James Robert Parish wrote, "As a botched blend of Hong Kong filmmaking and American quickie moviemaking, *Dragon Fight* did not do much to enhance Jet Li's stalled acting career."[44] However, the movie did change Li's life. During production, Li fell in love with his co-star Nina Li Chi, a former Miss Asia beauty queen. He decided to divorce his wife to be with Chi, who had returned to Hong Kong after the film was completed. Li has explained that he never really loved Huang and that his feelings toward Chi were so strong he had to be with her. Li said, "You realize, 'I can give up my fame and success, give up my status, give up my money. I'm even willing to die for her.' You realize this is love."[45]

Before Li returned to Hong Kong he also made *The Master* with director Tsui Hark. The contemporary drama shot in Los Angeles featured martial arts but was such a weak effort that it was not released until 1992. Despite that, Li's luck finally began to change because of Hark, one of Hong Kong's most stylish directors. Hark had begun experimenting with a movie camera at age eight and studied film at Southern Methodist University and the University of Texas at Austin. He realized Li's star potential and believed Li was the perfect actor to help him in his dream of revitalizing the martial arts film genre by making better movies.

When Li returned to Hong Kong in 1990, the films he made with Hark finally helped him become a major star. Interestingly, Li's career path followed one similar to that of Bruce Lee, who after failing to make his mark in Hollywood pictures also returned to Hong Kong to achieve international attention.

*Director Tsui Hark, a prominent Hong Kong filmmaker, recognized Li's potential as a martial arts movie star. Their work together includes* The Master *and* Once Upon a Time in China.

## Movie Star and Chinese Hero

In Hark's 1991 film *Once Upon a Time in China*, Li played Wong Fei-hung, a doctor and martial arts expert born in 1857, who was a true-life Chinese folk hero because he protected the weak and helped the poor. Wong also tried to keep foreigners from taking advantage of poor Chinese, including Americans who in this period lured them to the United States with promises of wealth only to make them work in virtual slavery as laborers. One of the many thrilling, stylish fight scenes that made the movie successful was a re-creation of a legendary battle in which Wong, armed only with a staff, defeats thirty criminals on the docks of Canton.

*The movie poster for 1991's* Once Upon a Time in China *features Li as folk hero Wong Fei-hung. The success of the film and its sequels launched Li's stardom in Asia.*

Before filming began, Hark invited Li to his home and showed him a video of a lion slowly stalking its prey and intimidating it with its fierce presence. Hark told Li he wanted him to mimic the way the lion hunted to bring more drama to his fight scenes. Li instantly realized that imitating the lion's ritual of circling an opponent to frighten it before attacking could add excitement to his films. In discussing *Once Upon a Time in China*, Li described how this technique helped him:

> Look at the two main characters right before they begin fighting. Circling each other [and] you know that a battle is already underway. That's how I learned to view fight scenes from a different perspective. No longer were they just a series of physical movements. You had to take a step back and see the emotions.[46]

That was one of many ways in which Hark helped Li improve his acting and the way he staged fight scenes. Li starred in two sequels to *Once Upon a Time in China*. He left the series to make other movies but eventually returned for the sixth installment of one of the most popular series of martial arts films ever made. *Once Upon a Time in China* was the first of many films in which Li played historical or fictional characters who were Chinese patriots. Martial arts and movie expert Martha Burr said Li's heroic portrayal of Wong Fei-hung gave him the powerful screen identity he needed to become a star: "We've come to view Jet Li as the archetypal hero, whether Shaolin monk or [another character] whose difficult journey triumphs in good over evil."[47]

Li's new star power—he needed eight bodyguards and seven hundred policemen to protect him from fans when he visited South Korea to promote *Once Upon a Time in China*—helped him gain more creative control over his movies. In 1992 he started Eastern Production, a production company that collaborated with major Hong Kong movie studios such as Golden Harvest to make films. Li enjoyed the process of making films in Hong Kong because "Hong Kong is a tight little film community. We just pick up the phone, call the studios, say we want to make a movie,

# A Martial Arts Superstar

**E**ven though many of Jet Li's Hong Kong movies did not gain widespread distribution in the United States, the superb martial arts skills he displayed in them caught the attention of top movie critics. This is how *Time* magazine critic Richard Corliss once praised the phenomenal, gravity-defying physical movements that made Li's films so popular:

> A cool star in repose, Li in action is a hot one. It is a deep movie pleasure just to watch him scale a flight of stairs (in *The Bodyguard from Beijing*) by vaulting over a railing, taking a long, lithe step up and then pushing himself over the top rail. His martial poses, with their wonderfully expressive names (the Rotation of the Stars, the Essence-Absorbing Stance, the ever-potent Wonder Screw), have classical beauty and power. His spin-kicks flout all laws of physics, if not metaphysics; there's nothing like Jet Li in a foot fight. His slippered feet (in *Once Upon a Time in China 3*) vs. four baddies with sabers: no contest! Four other miscreants (in *Fong Sai-yuk 11*) rush at Li while he is holding a squirmy princess on a raft; he throws her high in the air, disarms the quartet and catches the girl before she falls. In *The New Legend of Shaolin* he fights off a dozen attackers with his infant son strapped to his back.

Richard Corliss and Jeffrey Ressner. "Fighter Jet." *Time International*, October 12, 1998, p. 68.

and it's 'Okay, good idea.'"[48] Making films in the 1990s, however, could be dangerous because Hong Kong criminal gangs known as triads had begun using their money and influence to enter the movie industry. It is believed that Li's manager, Jim Choi, was shot to death on April 16, 1992, for refusing to let a triad use Li in a movie. Li has never commented directly on Choi's death.

However, this is how he once described triad involvement in Hong Kong movies:

> When these bad guys would take a gun to rob a bank and fight with policemen, maybe they'd get money or lose their life. But if they put a gun to an actor's head and told them to make a movie for half their regular salary, it was very easy to make money. Easy for them. Difficult for us.[49]

Luckily, Li escaped further involvement with triads and continued to star in a series of hit films in which he played a variety of roles. In 1993's *Tai Chi Master*, he played a disgraced Shaolin monk seeking redemption. He costarred in that movie with Michelle Yeoh, who in 1997 gained international fame by appearing in a James Bond movie. In 1993 in *The Legend*, Li portrayed Fong Sai-yuk, who was key in stopping an attempt to overthrow China's emperor centuries ago. *The Bodyguard from Beijing* was a 1994 remake of the Kevin Costner film *The Bodyguard* in which Li's character protected a witness in a murder trial.

In 1994's *Fist of Legend*, Li portrayed Chen Zhen, another real-life Chinese hero who in 1937 defeated Japanese karate experts to uphold the honor of Chinese martial arts. Because the Japanese invaded China not long after the incident at the start of World War II, Zhen's heroics were seen as the symbolic beginning of the Chinese fight against Japanese aggression. The movie is considered a martial arts masterpiece as well as a dramatic commentary on the animosity that existed between Japan and China. Reviewer Bill Gibron wrote:

> It features Li in one of his most compelling and iconic roles. The main theme running through *Fist of Legend* is the unflinching hatred between the invading Japanese and the victimized Chinese. In fact, it's hard to differentiate which is more powerful—the anti-Japanese sentiment or the battles.[50]

The movie paid tribute not only to Zhen but to Bruce Lee, whose 1972 *Fist of Fury* dealt with the same subject. Li had been compared to Lee ever since he began making movies because, unlike many actors in such films, they were both martial arts mas-

*Li, left, delivers a kick during a fight scene from 1994's* Fist of Legend, *in which he plays Chinese martial arts hero Chen Zhen. Most of Li's early movies saw him portray characters who were Chinese patriots.*

ters. Li wanted the world to know that, in making the movie, he was not trying to replace Lee in the hearts of his fans. Said Li:

> [Bruce Lee] is a hero over there [mainland China], just like everywhere else. Many young Chinese admire him and want to be like him. I'm not doing this film to say: "Hey look, here is the new Bruce Lee!" No, it's to show my respect for his memory.[51]

*Fist of Legend* and other movies added to Li's growing popularity in Asian countries, but he still wanted to achieve international stardom. To do that, Li had to appear in a movie made in Hollywood, the film capital of the world.

## Going to America

In *Once Upon a Time in China*, Li's character is told, "Everyone wears dark glasses in America because the gold the streets are paved with is so bright."[52] Li knew that riches and worldwide fame could be his if he could make a successful film in the United States. In 1998 Li finally got the opportunity he had sought for so long when he was asked to make his American film debut in *Lethal Weapon 4*. The movie would ignite Li's rise to international film stardom.

# Chapter 4

# An International Star

By 1997 Jet Li had become a major Hong Kong movie star and made enough money to feel financially secure for the rest of his life. Yet Li still dreamed of making movies in the United States because he wanted to act in films that would be seen worldwide instead of only in Asia. Li finally got that chance when he was asked to appear in the fourth installment of *Lethal Weapon*, a wildly successful series starring Mel Gibson and Danny Glover as police detectives whose exploits were both violent and funny. Li once explained how his dazzling performance in that movie led to a string of starring roles in films that made his name, face, and marvelous martial arts abilities known around the world:

> When I first came [to the United States] only the hard-core fans know Jet Li. Other people don't know who is that little Chinese guy. So you need to knock [on] the door, you hope the studio open the door for you. You need to come in to prove yourself. The next thing is [studio officials say] "Okay, you're not bad" so you get a leading role to do another movie. And you prove yourself again.[53]

Li's success in *Lethal Weapon* playing a supporting role to Gibson and Glover led U.S. studios to cast him in starring roles in *Romeo Must Die*, *Kiss of the Dragon*, and *Unleashed*, global hits that transformed Li into an internationally known movie star. But before that could happen, Li had to convince U.S. movie executives to give him a chance to show how good he was.

## Li's Big Hollywood Break

U.S. movie executives were intrigued by the star power Li had shown in making more than two dozen movies in the People's Republic of China (PRC) and Hong Kong. However, they were still not sure if Li had the screen charisma to make the jump to Hollywood, where the world's most prestigious films are created.

*The movie poster for Lethal Weapon 4 features Li, left, among its other high-profile American stars. Li's performance as the villain in the 1998 movie gave him his first big break onto the Hollywood film scene.*

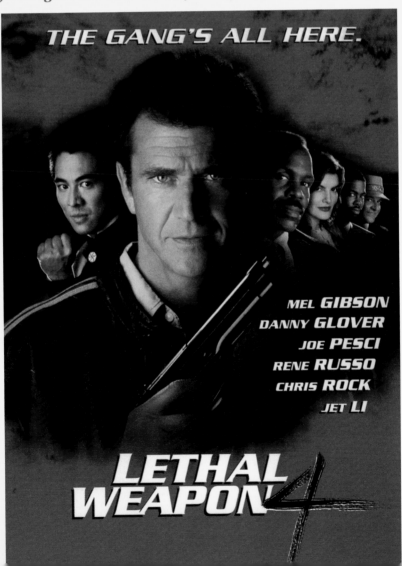

When director Richard Donner wanted to cast Li in *Lethal Weapon*, Warner Brothers studio made Li audition for the role by playing a scene with Gibson. Some established actors would have felt slighted at that request, but Li understood the studio's concern and agreed to do the screen test. Li said he and Gibson developed an instant liking for each other: "He's a very good man, have a wonderful heart, help me a lot. The language for sure, my English is little, but I have my heart."[54] Li's rapport with Gibson made for a solid screen test, and Li got the part.

Li's inability to speak fluent English was one of the concerns U.S. studios had about Li. In fact, his poor English had contributed to his failure to win any roles a decade earlier when he first tried to act in U.S. movies. So before filming started, Li and Nina Li Chi moved to Los Angeles so he could study English with a tutor. Li admitted later that the lessons were frustrating: "I use sentences 100, 200, even 300 times and still can't get them right. [Li thought,] I'm too old for this. I use a word in the wrong order in a sentence I get mad. It's very stressful."[55] While learning enough English for his lines in the film, Li also practiced martial arts eight hours a day to prepare for the most important film of his movie career.

In *Lethal Weapon 4*, characters played by Gibson and Glover try to break up a Chinese gang that is smuggling people illegally into the United States and forcing them to work as slave laborers. Li played Wah Sing Ku who was a "snakehead," the name for someone in charge of such a smuggling operation. For the first time in his movie career, Li was cast as the movie's villain instead of its hero. Li prepared for the part by trying to understand the mentality of a criminal. He decided that a villain would think positively, not negatively, about his actions even though they are evil: "I never think that a villain thinks, 'I am the villain.' In real life, the bad guy never thinks he's the bad guy. He just thinks, 'I need to do that. It's my job.'"[56]

Li's attempt to psychologically understand a Triad gangster helped him create a riveting portrait of merciless evil and a character whose menacing stare was as intimidating as any of the exotic kicks and punches he threw in the film's many fight scenes.

# A Breakout Performance

Gibson and Glover are both big, strong, and athletic, which made it seem believable in previous *Lethal Weapon* movies when they over-powered criminals they were trying to arrest. The fourth installment in the series, however, pitted them against a diminutive foe capable of beating the two larger actors to a bloody pulp at the same time. Donner had wanted someone like Li as the villain because he believed his exotic fighting skills would add a new level of action to the long-running series. But when the film debuted on July 10, 1998, Li made an impact on moviegoers not only with his dazzling wushu moves but the frightening menace his character projected.

In Li's first fight, he punishes a Triad member who allowed Gibson and Glover to capture a boat loaded with illegal immigrants. Clad in a black, high-collared suit, Li calmly fingers Buddhist prayer beads with one hand while easily beating his opponent senseless with kicks and punches. Li then pushes the beads to one side, exposing a wire he uses to strangle the criminal. The ease with which Li defeats someone who had earlier beaten Gibson in a spectacular fight and the deadly aura of evil Li radiated made his character come alive for people watching the movie. Li was such a whirling, kicking, punching weapon of destruction that reviewer Brent Kliewer labeled him "a one-man lethal weapon, giving (Gibson) and (Glover) all they can handle."[57]

Li's impressive martial arts skills gave the film the new level of excitement Donner had sought, leading him to proclaim ecstatically, "This is the best of the west meets the best of the east."[58] But Donner later admitted Li was so incredibly fast that the camera crew had trouble capturing his lightning moves on film. Li had several extended fights with Gibson, and Donner admitted that Li's quickness made it hard for Gibson to react to what Li was doing:

> Mel is fast, is quick, he loves to do his own stunts. And yet when he did the fights with Jet, Jet was so fast that Mel couldn't react to the punches, they were coming so fast. So

he had to memorize the fight moves. And not even looking at what was coming he would just throw his body in the direction they were coming. Jet was too fast.[59]

In the movie's climactic fight in a decrepit waterfront warehouse, Li has knocked out Glover and is slowly beating Gibson to death.

*Li's Lethal Weapon 4 **character, smuggler Wah Sing Ku, holds a set of Buddhist prayer beads that he uses to strangle his enemies.***

Glover revives enough to grab a yard-long, sharply pointed metal rod and jam it through Li's mid-section. Despite being impaled by the spike, Li continues to battle Gibson. When they fall off a dock into the water, Li nearly chokes Gibson to death until Gibson miraculously finds a machine gun that had fallen in the water. Gibson then uses the gun to kill the seemingly super-human Li.

Donner, a revered director of action films, praised Li's acting as well as his fighting skills: "I knew I was getting a genius in martial arts, but I also got a really sensational young actor."[60] Although some critics panned the movie by claiming its stars and the formulaic elements of the decade-old series were both getting old and tired, it debuted as the number one movie in the United States. But even reviewers who did not like the movie were impressed with Li's portrayal of a vicious Chinese Triad member.

Li's smash debut led to starring roles in *Romeo Must Die* and *Kiss of the Dragon*, movies that solidified his credentials as an actor famous and talented enough to help a film become a worldwide hit.

## A Leading Man

In 2000 Li starred in *Romeo Must Die* with Aaliyah, a popular R&B singer making her screen debut. Stealing the plot from Shakespeare's *Romeo and Juliet*, the movie has Li and Aaliyah fall in love even though they are on opposite sides of a battle between Asian and African American gangs who are fighting for control of crime in a U. S. city. The complex plot that brings them together allowed Li to exhibit his fantastic fighting abilities and Aaliyah to sing several songs.

Li's martial arts ability was augmented by extensive use of wires to help him and other actors do physical feats that are impossible for humans to perform. Wirework—the use of wires attached to harnesses to make actors appear to fly or float through the air—was a staple of martial arts movies, and it had been popularized recently in *The Matrix*, a wildly successful science fiction movie. Although some reviewers criticized *Romeo Must Die* for using too much wirework and other special effects, Bob Graham loved it. In his review in the *San Francisco Chronicle*, Graham wrote: "When

*A spectacular fight sequence between Russell Wong, left, and Jet Li in* Romeo Must Die *was enabled by wirework, which enhanced actors' ability to do amazing physical feats.*

Li rises in a long leap and plants kicks on four opponents in a row, it is a 'Matrix' moment."[61]

Li, however, has always favored realistic fight scenes except in period films about wushu heroes of the distant past who were said to have fantastic powers, such as being able to climb up walls or leap great distances. In the 2001 film *Kiss of the Dragon*, Li returned to this more realistic fighting style. He explains why he preferred that way to stage film fights:

After 'The Matrix,' everybody do action movie with people fighting while flying around. Suddenly everyone can fight. Man can do, girl can do, little boy can do, even cartoon [character] can do the same thing. In this movie, everyone really can do.[62]

In the movie Li plays an intelligence agent from the PRC who goes to Paris to arrest a Triad leader. The movie's plot came from a story Li wrote. In the film Li saves actress Bridget Fonda from being killed by Chinese gangsters and then engages in a series of spectacular fights before he finally arrests the Triad leader. For the movie, Li gave his character a unique martial skill—the ability to kill someone by sticking an acupuncture needle in a particular spot in their neck. The deadly technique was known as "kiss of the dragon," which became the movie's title.

# Bridget Fonda and Jet Li

**A**ctress Bridget Fonda was Jet Li's co-star in *Kiss of the Dragon*. Fonda comes from a famous acting family––her father, Peter, starred in the motorcycle classic, *Easy Rider*, and her aunt Jane has won two Oscars—and has appeared in many films with other well-known actors. Fonda claims that while they were shooting the film, she realized that Li's martial arts expertise helps make his character believable to the audience. Fonda said that is because, when Li is in a fight scene, he is not acting but doing what comes naturally to him after years of practicing the martial arts:

*Li and costar Bridget Fonda, right, appear at the premier of* Kiss of the Dragon. *Fonda praised Li's performance in the film.*

I find him to be a very interesting combination of things. He's completely intriguing. First of all he's really attractive. He also as a person is very shy. He's very shy, he's very strong. He's also lethal. So he is acting on the one hand, creating a character and on the other hand he's doing something that's absolutely real. He's s the real deal. He's really a martial artist in real life. We're not talking special effects, we're not talking what the camera can make it look like. You realize he's been doing that his whole life. It's inherent, it's automatic.

*Kiss of the Dragon*, 98 minutes, "Jet Li Featurette," Twentieth Century Fox Home Entertainment, Beverly Hills, CA, 2001.

Although critics praised Li's acting and martial arts ability in both films, the movies failed to bolster his romantic credentials. Li admits, however, that he would rather fight someone twice his size than kiss a beautiful woman because love scenes make him feel uncomfortable: "I can feel very brave through all the action scenes in front of the people who are on the set but when a girl comes close to me my face turns red because I'm so shy."[63] In real life, however, Li in this period proved that romance was important to him.

## Keeping His Promise

When Li divorced his first wife in 1990 to be with Nina Li Chi, he was hesitant to marry again too quickly. Li told Chi he would marry her if they were still together ten years later or if they were going to have a baby. Li kept that promise by marrying Nina on September 14, 1999, in Los Angeles, while he was completing work on *Romeo Must Die*. Li also kept another promise he had made to her—that if she ever became pregnant he would stay at her side until their baby was born. Li did just that, and their daughter Jane was born on April 19, 2000. The couple had a second daughter, Jada, in 2002.

To keep that second promise, Li had to say no to a starring role in one of the most successful martial arts movies ever made—the 2000 film *Crouching Tiger, Hidden Dragon*, which won four Oscars and starred Hong Kong veteran actor Chow Yun-fat. Even though Li's good friend director Ang Lee had written Chow's role for him, he said it was an easy decision to say *no* to starring in a film everyone expected to be a blockbuster hit:

Ten years ago I promised my wife, I say we love each other, if we still do ten years later we'll be married, and if we have a baby I'll stop my working, and be with you until the baby is born. In your whole life you can find a lot of successful scripts, work with successful people. But in life, you need to really take responsibility to your family. And I thought that was more important than the movie.[64]

Li did not totally abandon his career during his wife's pregnancy. He had come to realize that the Internet was a good way to

*Li and his wife Nina Li Chi appear at a movie premier in 2003. Li turned down a role in the hit movie Crouching Tiger, Hidden Dragon in order to be with Nina during her first pregnancy.*

stay in contact with his fans all over world. Li developed his own website (www.jetli.com) and worked hard to make it a good one. When a reporter asked Li in April 2000, "How much time does a wushu martial arts star have for the Internet?," Li responded, "Between one and three hours per day."[65] For his website, Li wrote a series of essays about how he had spent his childhood learning the martial arts because he wanted his fans to know how hard he had worked to gain his fantastic fighting abilities. Li also answered online questions on nearly every topic imaginable. His willingness to communicate directly with the public created even more fans.

# Jet Li and Bruce Lee

Jet Li has never liked being compared to Bruce Lee, because he never tried to make himself a cinematic copy of the legendary star. Such comparisons have been inevitable, however, because their names sound alike, they were both real-life martial arts masters, and their careers followed similar paths. In an article praising Li's movies, film critic Richard Corliss wrote that this lingering connection to Bruce Lee has even followed Li into movies he makes:

> At least there's something tonic about the films Li has made in the West. His character is so solid, so stolid that cross-cultural jokes fizzle around him; producers have stopped trying to turn him into a smiling Jackie [Chan] type. And since his mission is not to learn American ways but just to catch the damn villain, a Li movie can get down to basics: punch, kick, pummel, kill. In other words, Hollywood thinks Jet Li is the new Bruce Lee. In the Jetster's major-studio debut, *Lethal Weapon 4*, Mel Gibson glanced at Li's designer tunic and cracked, "Nice pajamas, Bruce." In [*Cradle 2 Grave*], Li still has to fend off references to Hong Kong's seminal martial artist, who died 30 years ago. An angry dwarf threatens to have his henchmen "kick your ass, Bruce." Li's response may be directed as much to his [movie] bosses as to the dwarf: "I'm not Bruce," he says wearily.

Richard Corliss. "The Tone Is Jet Black." *Time*, March 23, 2003. www.time.com/time/magazine/article/0,9171,436033,00.html.

## More Hit Movies

As Li's fame and popularity grew, so did his bank account. Li had earned only $750 for his first film, but he received $2.4 million for *Romeo Must Die* and $5 million for *Kiss of the Dragon*. When Li returned to acting after his daughter was born, he was paid

$7.5 million for *The One*, a quirky 2001 science fiction film in which he has to battle for survival against an evil twin from an alternate universe. In the film Li plays both the movie's hero (Gabe Law) and villain (Gabe Yulaw), who are two of more than one hundred copies of the same person who live in more than one hundred alternate universes that exist in other dimensions. When Yulaw gains the ability to travel between those dimensions, he starts killing his look-alikes because he believes he can become supremely powerful if he kills them all. Yulaw finally meets his match in Law, a Los Angeles County sheriff.

The movie's fight scenes are unique in that Li has to keep fighting himself. Even with the help of special effects, it was challenging for Li to shoot intricate martial arts battles in which he played both parts. Said Li:

> Yes, I've made a lot of films, but this is the hardest. Usually I play the good guy and I fight with the bad guy. Now, I need to fight with the stuntman, and when I finish my part I have

*Li and veteran actor Morgan Freeman, right, appear in the 2005 movie* Unleashed. *In the film, Li's character transforms from a brutal killer into a gentle soul.*

to turn back to be the bad guy, and fight the stuntman again. Sometimes you hit the bad guy, and the stuntman turns around and hits you. So, it's quite hard [Li starts laughing] to do everything.[66]

Playing multiple roles was the hardest part of making *The One*, but four years later Li faced an even stiffer challenge in *Unleashed*. In that movie Li played Danny the Dog, who was brutally raised since childhood by the head of a criminal gang (Bob Hoskins) to be an enforcer who would never hesitate to beat up or kill anyone. A chance meeting with a blind piano tuner (Morgan Freeman) makes Danny realize there is a better way to live. Although the movie has great fighting sequences, the underlying story of how music and kindness from a stranger transforms Danny's personality make the film a strong drama. Li said he fell in love with the movie because it had a positive message instead of merely being a vehicle to showcase the martial arts: "It's a different kind of action drama. I try to show that violence is not the only solution. Danny is physically very tough, but he doesn't like that kind of life."[67]

Action, not acting, had always been the main attraction of Li's films. Thus it was intimidating for him to work with Hoskins and Freeman, who were both highly respected for their acting ability. Li's role required him to act at a deeper level than he ever had before by showing how Danny, who begins the movie wearing a dog collar that symbolizes his brutal personality, evolves into a gentler person. Li said he learned how to express such deep emotions from watching Freeman, winner of a best supporting Oscar for *Million Dollar Baby*. Said Li:

Morgan Freeman, he made me believe every day I saw him [that I could act], I thought that's my uncle, that's my father, I want to hug him. I feel that's the way I can breathe and take some risks. Yeah, he showed me everything.[68]

# Getting Into Character

Jet Li knows many styles of martial arts. In his various movies, Li picks and chooses from those styles to make fighting scenes reflect the personality of the character he is playing. For *Unleashed*, Li tried to figure out how someone who was treated as an animal all his life would fight. Li explained this process in an interview for the movie:

> We needed to study to forget who Jet Li is. Danny is only mentally around 8 or 10 years old, so we need to forget a lot of information. [We] watched a lot of different kinds of dogs in the supermarket ... [and then] we tell Woo-Ping [who choreographed the movie's fight scenes] what kind of martial arts can we use to help him? You know, different personalities use different kinds of martial arts. Usually I play a bad guy, I have a bad guy style, and cop has a tough cop style. Usually, I have a Jet Li style with signature moves or something. But this time we try to do just like a dog in the beginning. Dogs, they didn't talk a lot, they only just use their eyes to show emotion, so when they fight it's very concentrated, simple. Look at you and punch! Punch! Punch! (makes sounds depicting a fight) until he feels safe and then go to the second one. That's how the martial arts were designed for this person.

Julian Roman. "Jet Li gets *Unleashed*!" *Movieweb.com*, May 11, 2005. www.movieweb.com/news/jet-li-gets-unleashed.

When *Unleashed* was released on May 13, 2005, Li received many favorable reviews for both his acting and martial arts prowess. Respected critic Roger Ebert wrote, "This is a story that could have made a laughable movie. That it works is because of the performances of Jet Li and Bob Hoskins."[69] Such praise was sweet for an actor more known for powerful punches than powerful performances.

# Jet Li the Philanthropist

It was like the scariest scene in any disaster movie ever made. A man, his daughters aged one and four, and the nanny who cared for them had just left the lobby of a luxury hotel in the Maldives Islands when they were engulfed by a giant wave, a tsunami created by an earthquake in the Indian Ocean. In an instant, the joyful family expedition to the nearby beach to swim and play became a fight for survival as the father desperately tried to prevent his children from being swept away by the powerful waves. The man was Jet Li, but he was not filming another hit movie. On December 26, 2004, Li was caught in a real-life disaster that killed eighty-two people and destroyed thousands of homes and businesses. Li at first was unsure how to save his daughters:

> When I looked back, everything I saw minutes ago was gone. Everything was surrounded by the ocean. The [nearby] houses collapsed. I continued to run but the water was already up to my mouth. I thought if the water rose another foot, what should I do? I was carrying my daughters and pulling my maid, do I let go or persist?[70]

In his movies, Li would have easily saved daughters Jane and Jada by himself. Instead, Li shouted for help, and four men helped him pull his children back to the safety of the Four Seasons Hotel. For the next few days until help arrived, Li, his wife, Nina, and daughters were trapped in the hotel without electricity, telephone

# A Tsunami Changes His Life

The tsunami that struck the Maldives Islands on December 26, 2004, and almost drowned Jet Li and his daughters Jane and Jada, changed his life. Even though Li and his daughters escaped unharmed, he was overcome by how helpless he had felt when the powerful waves had nearly carried his daughters away. He was also overwhelmed emotionally by the way the tsunami had shat-

*Survivors assess the devastation in a small Indian village after a series of tsunamis struck throughout Indonesia in December 2004.*

tered the lives of tens of thousands of people by destroying their homes and nearly everything they owned. Li explains that the widespread personal disaster the tsunami created made him realize he had a duty to help people less fortunate than himself:

> That day in the Maldives was a real turning point for me. I had spent the first 41 years of my life thinking about Jet Li first, wanting to prove I was special, wanting to prove I was a star. Everything I'd done was self-centered. In that lobby, however, I saw people of different colors, speaking different languages, helping each other. It was very much like in the movies, with people putting women, children and the elderly first, and I thought that if everybody helps, if everybody does a little bit, it will make a big difference.

Jet Li. "The Tsunami That Changed My Life." *Newsweek*, September 26, 2008. www.newsweek.com/2008/09/26/the-tsunami-that-changed-my-life.html.

service, and other essentials of daily life. Still, they were better off than local residents whose homes had been washed away and were frantically trying to find loved ones in the twisted wreckage the tsunami had left in its wake.

The tsunami was a life-changing experience for Li. In an interview, Li admitted, "When we came out from hiding [after several days], everywhere we went we saw death. I realized that life is unpredictable. I [decided I] want to spend the time I have [left in life] on [doing] things more meaningful."[71] Since the age of eight, Li had dedicated himself to learning the martial arts and making movies to earn money to take care of his family. Li was so grateful to have survived that he decided to help people whose lives had been shattered by devastating natural disasters.

## Helping People

Li donated $158,000 to tsunami victims. And in January 2005, Li announced he wanted to start a charity to help more people cope with such tragedies. He said his brush with death had given him the will and courage to start a project that he hoped would help people for years to come:

> Some things I dared not do in the past, I am ready to do them now. I really hope that this show of love for humanity will not be brief like a 100-meter race, but will persist like a marathon. I hope this will pass on for generations to come.[72]

On April 19, 2007, Li created the One Foundation. Li's global stardom led him to envision a relief agency that would aid survivors of natural disasters wherever they happened throughout the world. Li explained that his dream was based on the idea of people banding together as individuals to help each other: "The concept behind One Foundation is simple: 1 person + 1 dollar + 1 month (each month) = 1 (big) family [so that] everyone is connected as one world."[73] Li's foundation began raising money through individual contributions and fund-raising events to pay for emergency rescue operations, post-disaster recovery and disease prevention, and long-term support for victims of tsunamis, earthquakes, floods, and other natural disasters.

Li, right, appears with a wax likeness of himself at a 2010 event in Hong Kong to promote the One Foundation, a charitable organization he founded in 2007.

Li set up offices for his foundation in Hong Kong and the People's Republic of China (PRC) and said he planned to gradually extend its operations to other Asian countries and the rest of the world. Li's organization began working closely with the International Federation of Red Cross and Red Crescent Societies, the world's largest international relief agency, to provide aid to millions of people. The most massive effort Li's charitable foundation undertook was helping victims of the 2008 earthquakes in China's Sichuan Province that killed seventy thousand people and left hundreds of thousands of people homeless. Li was so stunned by the devastation in his homeland that he quit acting for most of 2008 to supervise distribution of $13.7 million in donations from his charity to earthquake victims.

*Prayer beads are visible under Li's collar at a movie premier in 2008. A devoted Buddhist, Li uses his movies to spread the positive lessons that his practice of the religion has taught him.*

In December 2008, Li visited Sanjian, which had been hit hard by the earthquake. When Li stepped out of one of eighteen SUVs in his convoy of relief vehicles, grateful residents of Sanjian gathered around him. Li explained to a reporter accompanying him that helping other people had become his main mission: "Philanthropy is my passion and my life now. I wake up and eat and I'm thinking about it. I'm still thinking in the bath. I talk to everyone I can."[74] The Red Cross honored the charitable work Li was doing on September 3, 2010, when it named him its first international goodwill ambassador. In January 2011, Li spent four days in Vietnam as an ambassador for the Red Cross to promote blood donations that were badly needed in that country. Also in 2011, the PRC acknowledged the good work his One Foundation was doing by registering it as a public foundation, a status that made it easier for the organization to operate in China.

Li's 2004 encounter with the tsunami directly ignited his drive to help other people. However, another part of Li's life had already provided him with the moral and spiritual foundation to undertake such selfless work—his deep belief in Buddhism and dedication to conducting his life by the principles that underlie that eastern religion.

## Li's Devotion to Buddhism

Buddhism is both a religion and a philosophy to guide the way people live. It essentially asks its adherents to avoid negative acts, such as violence and lying, and to treat everyone they meet with compassion and brotherhood. Li is often asked how Buddhism helps him in his daily life. The spiritual and religious concepts underlying Buddhist thought are complex, but Li usually tries to answer questions about Buddhism simply so people can understand what he means. This is how Li explained to a reporter how Buddhist beliefs help him live a better, happier life: "I don't think about the past or the future because I cannot control the result. I can only control myself. I just work every day to do my best. That's the Buddhist philosophy."[75]

Li was exposed to Buddhism when he met Buddhist priests while making his first movie at the Shaolin Temple. The priests saw so much spiritual potential in Li that they asked him to join their religious sect. The request horrified director Chang Hsin-yen, who anxiously told Li, "No, wait! Don't do that, we've got a movie to finish!"[76] Li declined that offer, but by the mid-1990s, he began seriously to study Buddhism. One of Li's spiritual masters is Lho Kunsang, a Buddhist from Tibet who is considered a holy man. Li chose him as a teacher despite the political tensions that exist between Tibet and Li's native China because the PRC used force in 1951 to seize control of the small country.

In 2003 Li explained how he had traveled to remote monasteries to study Buddhism: "In Tibet I was not able to shower for two weeks. There was no hot running water. But while I was there, I was truly happy."[77] Buddhism is something Li practices every day through prayer or meditation. During a 2007 interview, Li said that it is easy for him to make Buddhism a part of his daily life:

Really I would say, wherever I go, whenever I take the car somewhere or I get some coffee, I meditate every day. The longest I took [for almost constant meditation] was ten days in New York City in a temple. Ten days every morning from ten o'clock until ten o'clock at night, silent for ten days sleeping on the floor with a hundred people.[78]

Li's love of Buddhism is reflected in the prayer beads he collects as a hobby and which he used as a prop for the sadistic killer he played in Lethal Weapon 4. Li says with a grin "I collect them from all over the world. Sometimes I feel guilty spending the money. But I buy them anyway."[79] The beads help Li pray and concentrate while meditating, which both help make him calm and happy.

Buddhism began to mean so much to Li that in 1997 he considered retiring from making movies so he could practice it full time. But Lho Kunsang told him to use his fame as a movie star to help other people. Since then, Li has tried to use his movies to spread the positive messages he has learned from Buddhism: "So I try to teach. I try to say things now in my movies, more than just killing the bad guy, saving the day. That maybe fighting isn't the only answer. That's why I continue to work."[80]

# Jet Li's Buddhist Message

Jet Li's dedication to Buddhism almost led him to quit making movies in 1997 and devote his life to spreading its message around the world. Instead, Li decided he could best do that by continuing to act in films, because tens of millions of people saw all of his movies. On his official website, Li explains what he is trying to do:

> I had a responsibility to help introduce Buddhism to the West—in non-traditional ways and through non-traditional media. My main goal in making movies nowadays is not the movie itself. Instead, it is my hope to use the medium of film or TV or the Internet to share my understanding of Buddhism with those who are willing to listen. [I] just want to do my part to promote the Buddhist philosophy of loving-kindness and unconditional love, so that some can understand, even just a little, how to make the most of this human opportunity, this lifetime. I'm not trying to convert my audiences; I just want to offer information—to expose them to ideas they might not otherwise encounter. If they're not interested in the message, they may not even notice it. If they're ready to listen, they will.

Jet Li, "Jet's Personal Journey." The Official Jet Li Website: Spirit Essays." http://jetli.com/jet/index.php?l=en&s=spirit&ss=essays&p=4.

Li also wanted to make movies that showed the more serious, philosophical aspects of martial arts. One of Li's goals when he became an actor was to promote the martial arts because he believes they improve people's health and teach them important lessons about discipline and self-confidence. But after Li realized his films only glorified fighting ability, he decided to make movies that revealed the deeper meanings of martial arts. Thus Li's career as an actor began to become an extension of the beliefs that were already motivating his daily life.

## Messages in His Movies

In the 2002 movie *Hero*, Li played a character known only as "Nameless," an orphan who grew up to be a master fighter and swordsman and an official in a small province of China. Thanks to extensive wirework, the movie has some of the most thrilling, yet beautiful, fight scenes ever captured on film. In addition to fierce, realistic fight scenes, Li and his opponents, including several women, defy gravity while flying through the air and performing incredible maneuvers that lend the movie a mystical, magical quality. Li is killed at the end of the movie in a shower of arrows, but his death makes him a hero because it helps Qin Shi Huang unify China by becoming its first emperor. Respected film critic Roger Ebert, who is often critical of action films, gave it a glowing review: "A film like 'Hero' demonstrates how the martial arts genre transcends action and violence and moves into poetry, ballet and philosophy. It is violent only incidentally. What matters is not the manner of death, but the manner of dying."[81]

It was the movie's message that attracted Li to the film, the first he had made in China since the Shaolin Temple films that began his film career. Li said, "After reading [the script] I cried. It's the one I'm looking for a long time. I'm very proud of working on this film."[82] Li, who had always been a patriot, said that, despite its dramatic fight scenes, the movie had a much deeper meaning: "The message of *Hero* is that your personal suffering is not as important as the

*Li, left, battles actress Maggie Cheung in a dramatic fight scene from 2002's* Hero, *which depicts the unification of China under emperor Qin Shi Huang.*

suffering of your country."[83] When *Hero* was released in the United States in 2004, it became the nation's top movie, and it eventually earned more than $177 million around the world.

In the 2006 film *Jet Li's Fearless*, he played Huo Yuanjia, a famous and patriotic martial artist. In 1907, a time when foreign nations dominated China politically and economically, Huo defeated foreign fighters in a series of famous matches that helped people feel new pride in being Chinese. The movie is a story about personal redemption for Huo, who becomes ruthless and arrogant after achieving fame and fortune through his fighting prowess. Huo eventually realizes he has dishonored underlying principles of martial arts that his father taught him, such as honoring opponents,

# "I'm not a hero"

**M**illions of people in the world consider Jet Li a hero, either because they admire his martial arts prowess, enjoy watching movies he makes, or appreciate the work he is does helping other people. But Li is a humble person, and his personal philosophy rejects the idea that he is or even should be a hero to anyone. This is how Li explains his feelings on the subject of being a hero:

I'm not a hero. I just spent a lot of time learning martial arts. Maybe that's a unique thing. And I try to show you what I can do, but a lot of people can do it. I'm not anything special. So I never say I'm the best fighter in the world. You make enemies with your ego. I think a lot of guys on the street can beat me up. It doesn't mean anything. [I] Don't want to have a hero. When a hero comes, that means human beings have a problem. Bad things happen, and the hero comes to save everybody. I really hope there are no heroes in the world. If there are no heroes, that means we are safe.

Mike Zimmerman. "POW and ZEN." *Men's Health*, September 2004, p. 266.

and Huo becomes ashamed of himself. He retreats from public life and lives humbly for years until he realizes he must use his martial arts expertise to restore Chinese pride. Li claimed, "*Fearless* is actually about personal growth—about a guy who decides that in the end his greatest enemy is himself."[84]

In the many interviews Li gives as a global celebrity, he began to make positive statements about the martial arts. During interviews to promote *Fearless*, Li told reporters that wushu, the term for Chinese martial arts, is written using Chinese characters that can be translated as "stop" and "war." Li then claimed "Most martial-arts movies have forgotten about the stop. The most powerful part of martial arts is love. Compassion. Most martial-arts films are violence against violence."[85]

Li also began using such interviews to highlight causes he supports. Li contributed $62,500 from *Fearless* box office revenues to the Red Cross's Psychological Sunshine project, which promotes mental health. He had become interested in mental health after learning that more than 250,000 Chinese youth had committed suicide in 2003. Li said he wanted films like *Fearless* to show

*Li portrays Chinese martial arts legend Huo Yuanjia in Jet Li's Fearless, which was released in 2006.*

teenagers they could cope with deep depression just like Huo did when he became despondent over how his life had turned out:

> I want them to know that you cannot choose where you are born, but you can have the courage to make it to the end. I want to show the young people that there is a reason to keep going. They have to encourage themselves. They must find peace and balance.[86]

In a perfect world, Li might wish that every movie he makes would have a strong moral or ethical message about life or the martial arts. But even a star like Li has to accept roles in movies whose only purpose is to entertain people, and to the delight of his fans, he also keeps making such films.

## An "Emperor" and an "Expendable"

Li had memorable performances in two hit movies released in 2008—*The Mummy: Tomb of the Dragon Emperor* and *The Forbidden Kingdom*. The mummy film was the third in a comedy-adventure series starring Brendan Fraser as an archeologist who has to battle super-powerful villains who awake from the dead. Li played the first emperor of the Han Dynasty, who, when he comes back to life, has mystical powers including the ability to change into a giant dragon. Also in the movie was Michelle Yeoh, a martial arts expert, who was Li's co-star in *Tai Chi Master*. The movie earned more than $400 million worldwide but generally received bad reviews for failing to properly use Li's incredible martial arts talent. Typical of the critiques was that of Philip W. Chung in the San Francisco newspaper *Asian Week*:

> Why hire martial arts giants like Jet Li and Michelle Yeoh and not let them do what they do best? Li's character spends most of his time as a [special effects] creation [and when] the two do fight, it's mostly in brief sequences that do not do them justice. This is like hiring [famed composer Frédéric] Chopin and making him play "Chopsticks."[87]

The Forbidden Kingdom was a more positive outing as Li acted for the first time with Jackie Chan, a long-time friend and fellow Hong Kong martial arts star. Li played two parts—the Monkey King and a martial arts monk—in a complicated plot that involved teaching a teenaged American how to fight an evil warlord. Although fans of Li and Chan had both debated for years which one of them would win a screen fight, their one battle is inconclusive, and they later

*Li plays a reanimated leader from the Han Dynasty with mystical powers in* **The Mummy: Tomb of the Dragon Emperor,** *released in 2008. Although the movie was a box-office hit, critics gave it poor reviews.*

team up to help the teen defeat the movie's villain. *Newsweek* critic Rafer Guzman said it was a treat to see them together: "Thanks to the two stars' disparate styles—the laser-like focus of Li and the whirlwind whimsy of Chan—'The Forbidden Kingdom' makes up for its flaws with plenty of eye-popping moments."[88]

Both films were made before Li took time to help Chinese earthquake victims. The first movies he made after his philanthropic sabbatical were *The Expendables*, a fun-filled romp with fellow action stars Sylvester Stallone, Jason Statham, Dolph Lundgren, and Mickey Rourke; and *Ocean Heaven*, a low-budget Chinese-language drama in which Li plays a man who cares for his autistic son. The first film made more money, but the second was closer to Li's heart because of its message of parental love and sacrifice. During a visit to Hong Kong's Ocean Park to see dolphins with a group of mentally handicapped and autistic adults, Li said: "I hope everyone can examine what is the most important relationship in life—the relationship between parent and child."[89]

## A Humble Star

Family has always been important to Li, who often cites his gratitude for everything his mother and the father he barely knew did for him while he was growing up. Li is an internationally known celebrity, but he has never lost the humility that made him willing to endure endless hours of practice and hardship to learn wushu and then take on the new challenge of acting in movies. In discussing his life, Li likes to say he is "just a boy from China, a guy who has had special opportunities in the martial arts."[90] To the world, though, Li is much more than that—martial arts champion, movie star, and a small man with a large heart who works tirelessly to help other people.

## Introduction: A Gentle Action Hero

1. Quoted in Julie Jordan. "Jet Li." *People*, August 3, 1998, p. 29.
2. Jet Li. "Questions." *The Official Jet Li Website*. http://jetli.com/jet/index.php?l=en&s=body&ss=questions&p=x&date=001020.
3. Quoted in "A Kung Fu Swan Song." *Newsweek*, February 13, 2006, p. 48.
4. Quoted in Mike Zimmerman. "POW and ZEN." *Men's Health*, September 2004, p. 266.
5. Jet Li. "Questions." *The Official Jet Li Website*. http://jetli.com/jet/index.php?l=en&s=body&ss=questions&p=x&date=001020.
6. Quoted in Liam Fitzpatrick. "The Liberation of Jet Li." *Time*, December 2, 2008. www.time.com/time/magazine/article/0,9171,1862595,00.html.

## Chapter 1: Learning the Martial Arts

7. Quoted in Sean Macaulay. "I Get a Kick out of You." *The (London) Times*, November 8, 2001, p. 14.
8. Jet Li. "Life Essay." *The Official Jet Li Website*. http://jetli.com/jet/index.php?l=en&s=life&ss=essays&p=1.
9. Quoted in James Robert Parish. *Jet Li: A Biography*. New York: Thunder's Mouth, 2002, p. 13.
10. Quoted in William Nakayama. "Jet Li: The Chosen." *Goldsea Asian American Daily*. http://goldsea.com/Personalities/Lijet/lijet.html.
11. Quoted in Parish. *Jet Li*, p. 14.
12. Quoted in William Nakayama. "Jet Li: The Chosen."
13. Jet Li. "Life Essay: Part 2." *The Official Jet Li Website*. http://jetli.com/jet/index.php?l=en&s=life&ss=essays&p=2.
14. Quoted in William Nakayama. "Jet Li: The Chosen.".
15. Quoted in Gerri Miller and Jeanine Detz. "Off the Chain." *Joe Weider's Muscle & Fitness*, May 2005, p. 40.

16. Quoted in Charles Holcombe. "Theater of Combat: A Critical Look at the Chinese Martial Arts." *Historian*, May 1990, p. 411.

17. Jet Li. "Life Essay: Part 3." *The Official Jet Li Website*. http://jetli.com/jet/index.php?l=en&s=life&ss=essays&p=3.

18. Quoted in Parish. *Jet Li*, p. 21.

19. Jet Li. "Life Essay: Part 4." *The Official Jet Li Website*. http://jetli.com/jet/index.php?l=en&s=life&ss=essays&p=4.

20. Quoted in Jet Li. "My Instructor Wu Bin." *Beijing Wushu Team*, March 19, 1998. www.beijingwushuteam.com/articles/wubin.html.

21. Quoted in Martha Burr. "The Jet Li Story." *Kungfu*, May 1998. http://ezine.kungfumagazine.com/print.php?article=82.

22. Quoted in Julie Jordan. "Jet Li." *People*, p. 29.

## Chapter 2: Li Becomes an Actor

23. Quoted in David A. DeVoss. "Ping-Pong Diplomacy." *Smithsonian*, April 2002. www.smithsonianmag.com/history-archaeology/pingpong.html.

24. Quoted in William Nakayama. "Jet Li: The Chosen."

25. Jet Li. "Life Essay: Part 5." *The Official Jet Li Website*. http://jetli.com/jet/index.php?l=en&s=life&ss=essays&p=5.

26. Jet Li. "Life Essay: Part 7." *The Official Jet Li Website*. http://jetli.com/jet/index.php?l=en&s=life&ss=essays&p=7.

27. "Jet Li (age 11) meets President Nixon in the White House Rose Garden." *YouTube.com*. www.youtube.com/watch?v=uFULOB5sLio.

28. Quoted in Liam Fitzpatrick. "The Liberation of Jet Li."

29. Quoted in Parish. *Jet Li*, p. 25.

30. Quoted in William Nakayama, "Jet Li: The Chosen."

31. Quoted in Parish. *Jet Li*, p. 27.

32. Quoted in Martha Burr. "The Jet Li Story."

33. Jet Li. "Life Essay: Part 10." *The Official Jet Li Website*. http://jetli.com/jet/index.php?l=en&s=life&ss=essays&p=10.

34. Quoted in Gerri Miller and Jeanine Detz. "Off the Chain." *Joe Weider's Muscle & Fitness*, May 2005, p. 40.

35. Quoted in Barry Koltnow. "Where Bruce Lee Went, 'Kiss of the Dragon' Star Jet Li Follows." *Orange County Register*, July 6, 2001, p. 1.

36. Quoted in Martha Burr. "Jet Li Is Still the Hero: Kung fu and Hip-Hop Collide in Romeo Must Die." *Kungfu*, April 2000. http://ezine.kungfumagazine.com/magazine/article.php?article=114.

37. Quoted in William Nakayama. "Jet Li: The Chosen."

## Chapter 3: Hong Kong Movie Star

38. *Jet Li Superstar 8 Film Collection: Li-Thal Weapon.* Asia Vision, Hong Kong, July 6, 2010. (59:47).

39. Quoted in Martha Burr. "Big Jet Li Interview." *Kungfu*, November 2001. www.kungfumagazine.com/magazine/article.php?article=143.

40. Quoted in Parish. *Jet Li*, p. 49.

41. Quoted in Bret Fetzer. "Born to Defense—Jet Li Collection." *Masjo Movie.* http://movie.masjo.com/asian-movies/born-to-defense-jet-li-collection-2445.html.

42. Quoted in "Imported 1998: Jet Li." *People*, November 16, 1998. www.people.com/people/archive/article/0,,20126786,00.html.

43. Quoted in The Associated Press. "Jet Li Talks About His Two Marriages." *SINA*, November 28, 2005. http://english.sina.com/taiwan_hk/1/2005/1128/55809.html.

44. Parish. *Jet Li*, p. 62.

45. Quoted in "Jet Li Married First Wife to Change His Fortunes." *Talk Asia*, September 2, 2010. www.channelnewsasia.com/stories/entertainment/view/1078683/1/.html.

46. Parish. *Jet Li*, p. 71.

47. Quoted in Martha Burr. "The Jet Li Story."

48. Quoted in Olivia Rousset. "Kung phew." *Sydney Morning Herald*, May 12, 2000, Metro p. 9.

49. Quoted in Richard Corliss and Jeffrey Ressner. "Fighter Jet." *Time International*, October 12, 1998, p. 68.

50. Quoted in Bill Gibron. "*Fist of Legend* (1994)." *PopMatters*, September 7, 2008. www.popmatters.com/pm/post/fist-of-legend-1994.

51. Quoted in Martha Burr. "The Jet Li Story."
52. Quoted in Richard Corliss. *Time International*, p. 68.

## Chapter 4: An International Star

53. *Kiss of the Dragon.* "Jet Li Featurette." Twentieth Century Fox Home Entertainment, Beverly Hills, CA, 2001.
54. Quoted in Anjali Rao. "Jet Li: On-Screen Fighter, Off-Screen Peacemaker." *Talk Asia*, January 8, 2008. http://edition.cnn.com/2008/WORLD/asiapcf/01/08/talkasia.jetli/index.html.
55. Quoted in Stephen Short. "The World Is My Oyster." *Time* Web-Only Interview, April 12, 2000. www-cgi.cnn.com/ASIANOW/time/features/interviews/int.jetli.html.
56. Quoted in Parish. *Jet Li*, p. 144.
57. Brent Kliewer. "'Lethal 4': The Best in Series." *Santa Fe New Mexican*, July 17, 1998, p. 20.
58. *Lethal Weapon 4.* "Audio Commentary by Richard Donner." Warner Home Video, Burbank, CA, 1998 (127 minutes).
59. *Lethal Weapon 4.* Warner Home.
60. Quoted in Richard Corliss. *Time International*, p. 68.
61. Quoted in Bob Graham. "'Romeo Must Die' Flies on the Strength of Jet Li." *San Francisco Chronicle*, March 22, 2000. www.sfgate.com/cgi-bin/article.cgi?f=/c/a/2000/03/22/DD2174.DTL#ixzz0z9uI3Isl.
62. Quoted in Christopher Noxon. "Taking a Fast-Track Career in Stride." *Los Angeles Times*, July 4, 2001. http://articles.latimes.com/2001/jul/04/entertainment/ca-18244.
63. Quoted in William Nakayama. "Jet Li: The Chosen."
64. Quoted in Martha Burr. "Big Jet Li Interview."
65. Quoted in Stephen Short. "The World Is My Oyster."
66. Quoted in Martha Burr. "Big Jet Li Interview."
67. Quoted in Gerri Miller. "Off the Chain," p. 40.
68. Quoted in Julian Roman. "Jet Li Gets *Unleashed*!" Movieweb.com, May 11, 2005. www.movieweb.com/news/jet-li-gets-unleashed.
69. Roger Ebert. "Unleashed." *Chicago Sun Times*, May 12, 2005. http://rogerebert.suntimes.com/apps/pbcs.dll/article?AID=/20050512/REVIEWS/50504006/1023.

## Chapter 5: Jet Li the Philanthropist

70. Quoted in "Action Hero Jet Li Survives Tsunami." *Guelph Mercury* (Ontario), January 8, 2005, p. C9.
71. Quoted in Andrew Huang. "A Kung Fu Swan Song." *Newsweek*, February 13, 2006, p. 48.
72. Quoted in "Action Hero Jet Li Survives Tsunami." *Guelph Mercury* (Ontario), January 8, 2005, p. C9.
73. Jet Li. "ESSAYS: The One Foundation Project Page." *The Official Jet Li Website.* http://jetli.com/jet/index.php?l=en&s =spirit&ss=essays&p=8.
74. Quoted in Liam Fitzpatrick. "The Jet Age," p. 46.
75. Quoted in Gerri Miller and Jeanine Detz. "Off the Chain," p. 40.
76. Jet Li. "Spirit Essays: Jet's Personal Journey." *The Official Jet Li Website.* http://jetli.com/jet/index.php?l=en&s=spirit&ss =essays&p=4.
77. Quoted in "Simply the Best, A Portfolio of Men We Love." *People*, December 1, 2003. www.people.com/people/archive/ article/0,,20148754,00.html.
78. Quoted in Ben Johnson. "Jet Li Interview." *Martial Edge*, October 27, 2007. www.martialedge.net/articles/interviews-question-and-answers/jet-li-interview/.
79. Quoted in "Simply the Best, A Portfolio of Men We Love." *People*.
80. Quoted in Scott Bowles. "Chinese Action 'Hero' Jet Li Is a Thinker, Not a Fighter." *USA Today*, August 31, 2004, p. D3. www.usatoday.com/life/movies/news/2004-08-30-jet-li_ x.htm.
81. Quoted in Roger Ebert. "Hero." *Chicago Sun-Times*, August 27, 2004. http://rogerebert.suntimes.com/apps/pbcs. dll/article?AID=/20040826/REVIEWS/408260304/1023.
82. Jet Li. *Hero.* "Inside the Action: A Conversation with Quentin Tarantino and Jet Li." Miramax, Santa Monica, CA, 2004, 13:54.
83. Quoted in Liam Fitzpatrick. "The Jet Age," p. 46.
84. Quoted in Liam Fitzpatrick. "The Jet Age," p. 46.

85. Quoted in Rick Bentley. "'Fearless' Jet Li: Martial-Arts Actor Looks for Roles That Will Encourage Young People." *Fresno Bee* (California), September 21, 2006, p. 21.

86. Quoted in Rick Bentley. "'Fearless' Jet Li: Martial-Arts Actor Looks for Roles That Will Encourage Young People," p. 21.

87. Quoted in Philip W. Chung. "Jet Li and Michelle Yeoh: From 'Tai Chi Master' to 'The Mummy.'" *Asian Week*, August 1, 2008. www.asianweek.com/2008/08/01/jet-li-and-michelle-yeoh-from-tai-chi-master-to-the-mummy/.

88. Quoted in Rafer Guzman. "The Forbidden Kingdom." *Newsday*, April 18, 2008, p. 22.

89. Quoted in "Jet Li Has High Hopes for Movie about Autism." *USA Today*, June 7, 2010. http://content.usatoday.com/communities/entertainment/post/2010/06/jet-li-has-high-hopes-for-movie-about-autism/1

90. Quoted in Parish. *Jet Li*, p. 190.

**1963**

On April 26, Li Lian-jie (Jet Li) is born in Beijing, capital of the People's Republic of China.

**1971**

Li begins training in wushu at an after-school program at the Beijing Sports School.

**1974**

Eleven-year-old Li wins the Youth National Athletic Competition for wushu athletes younger than eighteen; Li joins the newly created Beijing Wushu Team; Li travels to the United States in July and performs at the White House.

**1975**

Twelve-year-old Li wins the Men's National All-Around Championship, an event open to martial artists of any age; Li also wins the title in 1976, 1977, and 1978.

**1979**

Li retires from wushu competition after a severe knee injury; Li agrees to act in *Shaolin Temple*, his first film.

**1986**

Li acts in and directs *Born to Defense*.

**1987**

Li marries Huang Qiuyan.

**1988**

Li moves to the United States to try to win parts in American films but is unsuccessful.

## 1990

After making two movies for Hong Kong studios in the United States, Li divorces his wife so he can be with Nina Li Chi. Li returns to Hong Kong.

## 1991

The film *Once Upon a Time in China* is a huge hit and makes Li a major star in Asia.

## 1998

Li's role in *Lethal Weapon 4*, his first U. S. film, sets him on the path to becoming an international movie star. He becomes a global star with films such as *Romeo Must Die* (2000), *Kiss of the Dragon* (2001), *The Forbidden Kingdom* (2008), and *The Mummy: Tomb of the Dragon Emperor* (2008).

## 1999

On September 14 Li marries Nina Li Chi; they have a daughters, Jane, on April 19, 2000 and Jada, in 2002.

## 2004

On December 26, Li and his daughters Jane and Jada are nearly killed when a tsunami strikes the Maldives Islands.

## 2007

On April 19, Li creates the One Foundation, a charity to help people recover from natural disasters like tsunamis.

## 2008

Li quits making movies most of the year to concentrate on aiding victims of earthquakes in the People's Republic of China.

## 2010

Li stars in the action hit *The Expendables* and *The Ocean*, a Chinese-language drama about autism.

# For More Information

## Books

David Bordwell. *Planet Hong Kong: Popular Cinema and the Art of Entertainment*. Cambridge, MA: Harvard University Press, 2000. A book that explains the history of kung fu films made in Hong Kong, including some of Jet Li's movies.

Stefan Hammond. *Hollywood East: Hong Kong Movies and the People Who Make Them*. Chicago: Contemporary Books, 2000. The author explains how Hong Kong films are made.

James Robert Parish. *Jet Li: A Biography*. New York: Thunder's Mouth, 2002. This biography concentrates on Li's early film career.

## Periodicals

Martha Burr. "Jet Li Is Still the Hero—Kungfu and Hip Hop Collide in Romeo Must Die." *Kungfu,* April 2000. www.kungfumagazine.com/magazine/article.php?article=113. This article discusses Jet Li's movie career and how he approaches acting.

Martha Burr. "The Jet Li Story." *Kungfu*, October, 1998. www.kungfumagazine.com/print.php?article=82. An interesting biography about Jet Li by a writer who understands martial arts.

Richard Corliss and Jeffrey Ressner. "Fighter Jet." *Time International*, October 12, 1998, p. 68. This story has biographical material and explains how Jet Li achieved international stardom by making *Lethal Weapon 4*.

Jet Li. "The Tsunami That Changed My Life." *Newsweek*, September 26, 2008. www.newsweek.com/2008/09/26/the-tsunami-that-changed-my-life.html. An article Li wrote about how he and his daughters escaped the 2004 tsunami and how it changed his life.

Liam Fitzpatrick. "The Liberation of Jet Li." *Time*, December 2, 2008. www.time.com/time/magazine/article/0,9171,1862595,00.html. This article discusses Jet Li's charity work.

William Nakayama. "Jet Li: The Chosen." *Goldsea Asian American Daily*, http://goldsea.com/Personalities/Lijet/lijet.html. A fact-filled biography about Jet Li.

Anjali Rao. "Jet Li: On-Screen Fighter, Off-Screen Peacemaker." *Talk Asia*, January 8, 2008. http://edition.cnn.com/2008/WORLD/asiapcf/01/08/talkasia.jetli/index.html. In this wide-ranging interview on a Hong Kong talk show, Jet Li discusses topics from the movies he makes to Buddhism.

## Websites

**The Internet Movie Database** (www.imdb.com/name/nm0001472/). This site has information on Jet Li's movies and links to biographies and other information on the action movie star.

**Jet Li Facebook** (www.facebook.com/JetLi). Jet Li's Facebook site.

**Jet Li Fan Site** (www.jet-li.com/). This fan site has a biography and information about his movies.

**Jet Li's Official Website** (http://jetli.com). Jet Li's personal website is a wonderful source of information. It has a biography, videos, essays by Li, and answers he has written to questions from fans.

**New York Times** (http://movies.nytimes.com/person/42291/Jet-Li). This newspaper website has a biography, stories about Jet Li, and links to other sites about him.

Michael V. Uschan has written more than eighty books including *Life of an American Soldier in Iraq*, for which he won the 2005 Council for Wisconsin Writers Juvenile Nonfiction Award. It was the second time he had won the award. Uschan began his career as a writer and editor with United Press International, a wire service that provides stories to newspapers, radio, and television. Journalism is sometimes called "history in a hurry." Uschan considers writing books a natural extension of the skills he developed in his many years as a journalist. He and his wife, Barbara, reside in the Milwaukee suburb of Franklin, Wisconsin.